Complete Book of Linebacker Play

JOE GIAMPALMI

Parker Publishing Company, Inc.
West Nyack, New York

GV
951.18
.G52
1984

Library of Congress Cataloging in Publication Data

Giampalmi, Joseph
  Complete book of linebacker play.

  Includes index.
  1. Football—Defense.   2. Football—Coaching.
I. Title.
GV951.18.G52 1984   796.332'2   83-13437
ISBN 0-13-157511-2

Dedication

To my wife Madeline—thank you for reminding me
that life is much more than a shutout, quick out, back out,
and time-out.

FOREWORD

After coaching high school sports for more than forty seasons (half as assistant football coach, half as head baseball coach), I learned more than how to diagram plays in the snow, shower without hot water, dress warmly on a painfully cold day, dress coolly on a humid hot day, buckle a sweaty shoulder strap in twenty-five seconds, and give a homework assignment at 2:15 and catch the team bus at 2:30.

I learned that high school athletics offer hope for America's future, that more coaching hours isn't synonymous with more wins, that a low-keyed approach can be highly successful, that coaches are the best teachers, and that teenagers aren't as excited about sports as coaches are.

I also learned that each X and O is a unique, emotional human being, and the son of two proud parents. Two of those O's in Sun Valley's program are representative—my son, Joe, and Head Coach Bob Fithian's son, Rob. Coaching our sons caused us to evaluate every detail of our program: practice routines, drills, equipment, safety, conditioning, opponents, coach techniques, pressures, peer influence, and so forth. We didn't change anything. Joe and Rob complained that we treated them as badly as we treated the other players.

Joe and Rob are characteristic of approximately one thousand teenagers who have played for us since 1967 at Sun

Valley. Since they're also representative of most high school football players in the United States, I have confidence that America's future is secure because hundreds of thousands of high school football players are learning that:

- Success requires sacrificing.
- Ability and qualification earn respect.
- Teams can do what individuals can't do.
- Occasionally, best isn't good enough.
- A short cut is usually a wrong cut.
- God loves winners and losers.
- Better opposition develops better competition.
- The quest for perfection requires reevaluating and replanning.

I have less confidence in the future of the game itself. In the Pennsylvania, Delaware, New Jersey, and Maryland areas, interest in high school football is declining. Spectator support is waning, newspaper space is decreasing, costs are increasing, and school interest is apathetic.

On the field, offenses lack creativity, players' skills are decreasing, and coaching philosophies need questioning.

But we do have our strengths and school administrators should emulate our techniques for building successful programs because academics are underemphasized. Academics needs football's discipline, industriousness, enthusiasm, promotion, and competitiveness.

Administrators and teachers need to demand the respect that coaches demand. Lesson and curriculum planning needs the meticulousness of game planning and evaluating.

Schools have pep rallies to enthuse players prior to playing a big game. Has a school ever had a pep rally to enthuse students prior to taking the College Boards or exams? Coaches groups select and honor all-league and all-area players. Why don't schools select and honor the best students in English, science, and so forth? Why can't the best in the state be recognized? What newspaper wouldn't print a story recognizing the best foreign language students in the state? Academics should have active parent booster groups (not inactive PTAs) to promote, assist, and support learning. Some football parent groups (usually at a banquet) give a player a jacket for making a team. Homeroom teachers (usually while taking roll) give a student a three-by-five card for making the honor roll. Coaches promote a player who scores three touchdowns in a game; no one promotes a student who scores 1300 in the SATs.

While high school academics needs some improvements, high school football needs some restrictions. It needs shorter seasons, shorter practices, and fewer staff meetings. A season beginning the second week in August and ending the third week in November is too long. A three-week preseason practice period should begin the last week in August and an eight- to nine-game season should follow. Summer camp should be abolished and summer touch leagues (four weeks of playing tag football against other schools) should be eliminated. Also some schools practice too long and some staffs meet too long. High school players need time to be teenagers and high school coaches need time to be adults.

Another growing problem is parent booster groups. Parents who support their children are commendable, but supporting shouldn't include criticizing coaches, players, strategy, offenses, and defenses. Admirable players generally have admirable parents and problem players generally have problem parents. Also, the time that parents support their children athletically should at least equal the time they support them academically.

Regardless of high school football's problems, the game has a positive effect on the teenagers it attracts. Football is good for the very least it does—keep teenagers out of trouble while they're participating. Since most participants aren't problem people, football has the potential to produce proud, productive Americans.

If we as coaches believe in the values of our game, we will evaluate it and design a game plan for the future.

HOW THIS BOOK WILL IMPROVE YOUR LINEBACKERS AND STRENGTHEN YOUR DEFENSE

Coach, no matter how your defense shapes up now, this book will make it better! The *Complete Book of Linebacker Play* shows you how to improve your linebacker play and strengthen your defense. Effective defense depends on effective linebackers.

This book offers you the basic techniques of linebacker play that are applicable to almost any defense—odd or even, read or stunt, stacked or staggered. Whether you run a defense with one linebacker or four linebackers, this book has the right technique for *you!*

Everything you need to know about linebackers is here in this complete guide: how to align and where to stunt; how to drop on a pass and pressure on a run; the best way to read a trap and react to the draw; how to pursue the pitch and recognize the reverse; how to defend the run on the goal line and the pass on the sideline.

Complete Book of Linebacker Play is the product of my twenty years of high school coaching, learning, experimenting, failing, and succeeding. The linebacker techniques in this book have succeeded and are presently succeeding. They have helped Sun Valley High School (Aston, Pennsylvania) win five league championships and four second places, while averaging 3.5 yearly shutouts, including 7 (in ten games) shutouts one season.

The unique features of this book that helped produce those statistics are:

1. Linebacker keys for defending specific offenses such as the Veer, Pro, and Wing T (chapter 7 offers techniques and plans-of-attack)

2. Stunting techniques and tips that include when to stunt, where to stunt, and how to stunt

If stunting linebackers are part of your defense package, chapter 8 is custom-made for you. You'll learn how to percentage-gamble when you select the location to stunt your linebackers. This chapter also shows you stunting techniques that include crossing and picking, and using ins and outs. In addition, you'll learn how to disguise and bluff your stunts, two skills that complement your blitzes.

Other seldom-in-print information discussed in this book includes an outline of how to prepare your linebackers for weekly opponents. Linebacker mechanics have to be refined weekly to match your opponent's traits and tendencies. Chapter 9 tells you how to study your opponent's offense, scout that offense, and stop that offense.

After preparing your linebackers specifically for the expected, chapter 10 helps you prepare generally for the unexpected. Are your linebackers ready to defend an unusual spread formation? a huddle-less offense? a silent snap? Do you prepare on Wednesday rather than during a time-out on game day? What if you don't have a time-out or don't want a time-out? Chapter 10 answers these questions.

Coaches frequently ask if leaders can be made. Regardless of what you answer, a linebacker can be trained to call a defense confidently. You can train him to avoid prefacing a defensive call with "let's try." You can teach him (with the tips in chapter 11) to give encouragement and enthusiasm to other defensive players.

The completeness of the above topics and the depth of other subjects make this book different from other books written on the subject. All previously mentioned topics are discussed relative to all linebacker positions—middle linebackers, inside linebackers, weakside corners, and strongside corners. The depth of information for each of these positions includes keying, aligning, pursuing, pass dropping, and run pressuring.

In addition, the complete linebacker coverage of this book includes techniques for covering backs in pass patterns, shedding blockers, tackling safely, varying alignment, pressuring passers, reacting to the ball, defending action passes, reading the inside trap, reacting to the outside screen, playing a "half-corner" defense, defending the Veer with the help of an optical illusion, using the rulebook to play more aggressively, making desperation tackles, causing fumbles, playing the angles, keying uncovered linemen, and much, much more.

Finally, chapter 12 gives you dozens of drills for developing linebacker skills and techniques. You'll see illustrated drills for developing linebackers' agility, shedding, pursuing, stunting, reacting, keying, pass defending, and ball-handling. By drilling this book's skills and techniques, you'll improve your linebacker play and strengthen your defense.

It's all in your hands, the keys to developing outstanding linebackers who make outstanding plays, and the techniques for making your linebackers heard before they're seen. Read it, teach it, try it, and *win* with it!

Joe Giampalmi

ACKNOWLEDGMENTS

In addition to the people I acknowledged in *Complete Book of Defensive Line Play*, I'd like to especially recognize people who influenced my life and professional career.

First, I'd like to single out my parents. As I see more and more teenagers growing up with problems, I appreciate more and more the emotional stability they gave me—the happy childhood, the security, the education, the religious training, and the love. I grew up thinking a dad's job description included playing baseball every day, going to Phillies and Warriors games, attending Little League games, taxiing teams, and providing partial scholarships.

I'm thankful to my mother for wheeling me in a stroller to watch college football games, feeding pizza and spaghetti to every teammate I brought home, providing me with the cleanest uniform on every team I played, pinning medals inside every uniform I ever wore, and so many, many more acts of love.

I'd like to also thank my wife Madeline for her acceptance of me as a husband-coach, and for her regularly reminding me that the world does not exist on sports alone. Madeline, and our children Joe, Jeff, and Lisa are the inspiration behind everything I do.

Professionally, the content of this book could not be possible without the arguing between our Sun Valley staff:

Bob Fithian (head coach), Mike Lashendock, Bill Benedict, and Ron Withelder. Our combined years of coaching experience exceeds a hundred. That's near the experience needed to know that after winning, losing or tying; playing emotional, unemotional or emotionless; clinching a championship or securing the cellar—the only people always happy to see us after the game are our wives (Madeline, Karen Fithian, Sharky Lashendock, Ruth Benedict, and Shiela Withelder).

Our staff's success at Sun Valley would not have been possible without the dedication of the outstanding young men who played for us and without the cooperation of the Penn-Delco School District. Dr. John M. Cipollini and previous superintendents (the late Dr. Vincent Sauers and William G. Moser) have recognized the educational value of athletics. Another important person that has a direct influence on our success is our team physician, Dr. John G. Walichuck.

I'd also like to acknowledge Sister Ruth Schutz (Neumann College) and Dean Andrew Bushko (Widener University) who gave me the opportunity to teach freelance writing on the college level.

Finally, I'd like to acknowledge Parker Publishing Co., Inc. for their help writing this book and my previous book (*Complete Book of Defensive Line Play*). Parker's confidence in my football knowledge and writing ability has permitted me to fulfill a goal. I sincerely appreciate the editorial help and professionalism extended me by Jack Leach and Kathy Dix. They helped funnel many years of experience into a few hours of reading.

J. G.

CONTENTS

1

COACHING THE LINEBACKER'S STANCE AND START

Effective linebacker play begins with a good stance and a quick start. After your linebackers develop a good stance, you can help them start quickly by varying their alignment, making them more difficult to block.

Essentials of a Good Stance

A good stance is essential to any position in football, because a player cannot start quickly without it. The basics of a good linebacker stance are the correct positioning of head, arms, knees, and feet.

The position of the head establishes the path that the rest of the body follows. Since you want your linebackers' initial movement to be forward (to defend run first), the head should be leaning forward, toward the line of scrimmage.

If the head is leaning forward, the body weight will also be forward and the arms will hang freely. Elbows should bend slightly, anticipating the ninety-degree position necessary for shedding blockers.

A fault of many inexperienced linebackers is resting their hands on their knees, causing the elbows to lock. This resting position delays reacting to a key because it necessitates a preliminary shifting of the weight off the knees prior to the first reaction step. Also, the arms are not positioned for shedding.

Another stance fault is standing upright, which makes the linebacker blockable and less mobile. Backers stand higher as they tire and lose intensity. An upright linebacker is a coaching clue that the defense is losing momentum.

Proper positioning of the knees reduces the blocking surface that linebackers expose to offensive linemen. Knees should be slightly flexed, protruding forward. The distance between the knees should be about the same as the distance between the feet. Feet should be positioned parallel with a slight stagger for pushing off.

A good stance is a prerequisite to getting a good start and delivering a strong hit. Linebackers should maintain the hitting position from the time the offense breaks the huddle until a few seconds after the whistle (to protect against the late hit).

Getting a Quick Start

A good stance helps a quick start. You want your linebackers to get a good start by reacting quickly to their keys.

A good start begins with a survey of the situation while the opponent is huddling and aligning. In addition to linebackers knowing the obvious (down, distance, field position, game conditions), they should also know the location of the offensive backs and the location of uncovered offensive linemen.

Also, your linebackers must know their major and minor responsibilities for run and pass, and they must be thinking of those responsibilities in relation to the situation. Linebackers must anticipate reacting to situations similar to the following:

Run situation—Who are the opponent's best runner and best blocker? What are run tendencies for formation and field position? Are any offensive linemen keying through communication while leaving the huddle?

Pass situation—Who are the opponent's best passer and best receiver? Is the passer right-handed or left-handed? What are pass tendencies for formation and field position?

A quick mental survey of the situation (similar to above) prepares the linebacker to react quickly to the play. After making this survey, the linebackers must review their responsibilities. For example, if a linebacker anticipates a pass situation, he must consider:

1. The pass keys he will react to (uncovered linemen, a back or combination of backs, the ball, etc.)
2. Pass-drop responsibilities
3. Responsibilities for variations of a pass play (screens and draws)
4. Responsibilities for a play other than a pass

The first responsibilities a linebacker should look for are those prepared in the game plan. If the offense aligns with a tight end and a wing on the same side, and the game play says they like to run that side, the linebacker should be thinking and looking for that play first. (Chapter 9 discusses the use of defensive audibles to defend strong tendencies.)

Whatever the key or responsibility, linebackers must start quickly. That quick start results from an impulsive reaction to the initial movement of an offensive lineman. If a linebacker is aligned off the center, the defender should react to the movement of the ball. If a linebacker is aligned off a guard or tackle, he should react to the movement of the offensive lineman's hand.

Linebackers cannot react to offensive backs because a back's movements are not required to coincide with the snap of the ball. Consequently, a back shifting or motioning would draw a linebacker offsides.

Avoid inadvertently teaching your linebackers to go offsides by drilling them to react to sound (including a whistle). Prior to a crucial snap, your linebackers may prove how well you trained them to react to sound.

Varying Alignment

Linebackers can get a quick start and a defensive advantage by varying alignment. Decoy alignments frequently confuse rule-blockers and often force the offense into poor blocking schemes.

When linebackers and defensive linemen coordinate varying alignments, the offensive linemen must often read blocking assignments as the play progresses. Varying alignment creates an offensive problem such as a blocker's rule dictating his blocking a man aligning in a gap, but when the offensive lineman steps to the gap, the defender slants to head up and a linebacker slides over.

Figure 1-1 shows varying alignments for a middle linebacker (assigned to align off the center) and two guards assigned to hit head up. In these various alignments, the down linemen hit head up on the snap, and the middle linebacker slides to align off the center.

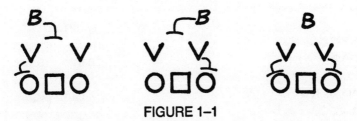

FIGURE 1–1

When you give your linebackers and linemen freedom to vary their alignments, make sure you set limits on the distance they may align away from their assigned area.

2

MAKING A
MIDDLE LINEBACKER

A quick-starting, aggressive middle linebacker makes an average defense good and a good defense outstanding. His good play strengthens your run defense from sideline to sideline and strengthens your pass defense from hook zone to hook zone.

Alignments

The common alignments for middle linebackers are head off the center or head off an uncovered offensive guard (see Figures 2-1A and 2-1B).

The depth of a middle linebacker's alignment is dictated by the opponent's offense and your style of defense. If you're defending an option offense, a deeper alignment (4 yards) permits time to read and react to an option give or a

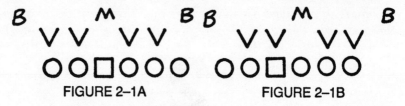

FIGURE 2–1A   FIGURE 2–1B

fake give. The read is made while the linebacker is moving toward the line of scrimmage.

This deep position also gives him extra thrust to shed a blocker or make a tackle. In addition, his depth discourages him from committing a linebacker no-no—moving backward on a running play.

If you run a predominately stunting defense, you want your linebacker closer to the line of scrimmage (1 to 2 yards), reducing the distance between the alignment and the offensive backfield. Another advantage of a tight alignment is that the linebacker is nearer to closing holes and limiting a back's area of maneuverability.

Keying

Alignments for middle linebackers may vary, but run responsibilities are constant. He must stop inside runs including:

sneaks

dives

counters

draws

inside reverses

inside traps

Middle linebacker keys include variations of the triangle formed by the quarterback and two running backs. An additional key is reading that triangle through the center and offensive guards. These middle linemen show plays by their blocking patterns. Combination blocks among the three indicate a play being run up the middle. These blocking schemes include crossing (Figure 2-2A), traps (Figure 2-2B) and reach blocking (Figure 2-2C).

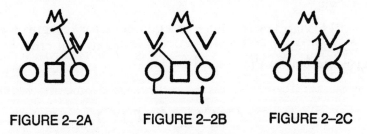

FIGURE 2–2A   FIGURE 2–2B   FIGURE 2–2C

Run keys shown by the offensive backs include:

1. Both backs moving in the same direction
2. Crossing action
3. One back faking outside and the other back running inside
4. One back diving and the other running outside

Before reading any combination of keys, a middle linebacker must look for a quarterback sneak. Overlooking this basic play can lead to a defensive disaster.

An equally dangerous middle play, but more difficult to read, is the inside reverse. This play will develop similar to an outside play or an off-tackle play and the middle linebacker can easily react incorrectly to the fake part of the play. Correct reverse reaction requires reading between the lines and recognizing additional keys such as:

1. Knowing previous game situations when the opponent has reversed
2. Recognizing lazy faking of the initial part of the play

3. Seeing a wingback running inside

4. Observing a wingback aligning deeper than usual

5. Hearing a defensive lineman yelling reverse when the wingback starts inside

6. Knowing that teams rarely run a wingback inside and not give him the ball

This last key is similar to a guideline for recognizing inside counters (see Figure 2-3)—most teams that cross backs give the ball to the second back.)

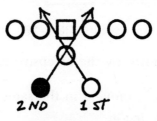

FIGURE 2–3

Verify this key in your scouting. Look to see if your opponent crosses backs and gives the ball to the first back. If they don't hand off to the first back, you can tell your middle linebacker that whenever backs cross, the second back will get the ball.

After recognizing a counter, reverse, or any other inside play, a middle linebacker has to pursue to make the tackle.

Pursuing Inside Plays

Since the middle linebacker's primary responsibility is stopping the inside run, you should design your defenses so that he has only one offensive lineman to beat to pursue the inside run. Try to avoid giving that uncovered blocker an angle block on your middle linebacker.

To beat that one blocker (usually the center), the middle linebacker has to contact him head-on, defending both sides of the blocker. If an offensive blocker tries to angle block the middle linebacker, the defender must fight through the blocker, attacking the blocker's shoulder nearer the ballcarrier. A common technique for beating an attempted angle block is the linebacker delivering a shoulder lift. (See "Shedding," chapter 5.)

Shedding the blocker and pursuing inside plays requires the middle linebacker always to move toward the line of scrimmage on running plays. A major error of middle linebacker play is moving backward on an inside running play. Moving backward not only makes an easy block, but it also creates a bubble in the defense, giving the runner a hole to break right or left. (See Figure 2-4.)

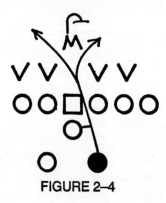

FIGURE 2–4

After moving forward and shedding blockers, the middle linebacker has to sight and pursue a collision course with the ballcarrier. When the middle backer pursues between the tackles for the ballcarrier, the backer should aim for contact on the carrier's inside shoulder. This angle positions the linebacker for a cutback and reduces chances of overrunning the play.

A major linebacker fault is overrunning the ballcarrier, making the defense powerless against the cutback. Ballcarriers are drilled to look for the cutback. Linebackers must be drilled to stop the cutback.

If your middle backer is taking too deep a pursuit angle, the problem may be your defensive linemen being blocked back a few yards.

Your linebackers need room to roam. They must have freedom of mobility without the hazards of the heels of your defensive linemen. To allow your linebackers this freedom, defensive linemen must make offensive contact in the neutral zone. If your opponent's offensive line dominates your defensive line, your defensive line will cut off the pursuit of your linebackers.

Pursuing Outside Plays

Keys for a linebacker to recognize an outside play include:

long yardage
hash-mark tendency
strong formation to the wide side
lineman tipping an outside pull
back cheating outside

The long yardage key is the most obvious indication. On second and long and third and long, the middle linebacker can cheat back 2 to 4 yards, giving him better leverage outside and a start into the hook zone. This extra depth alignment sacrifices a few running yards on quick dives, but the long yardage situation allows a few yards to be given up.

The important coaching point for pursuing outside is teaching linebackers to angle where the ballcarrier will be, and not to angle where the ballcarrier is seen. If middle backer (or any defender) pursues an angle where he sights the ballcarrier, the ballcarrier will outrun the angle. (See Figure 2-5.) Many linebackers misjudge outside pursuit angles because they:

1. Underestimate the ballcarrier's speed, and
2. Overestimate their own speed.

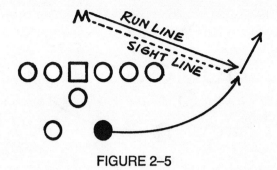

FIGURE 2–5

A good coaching guideline is to teach middle linebackers to aim for an angle 5 to 6 yards in front of the ballcarrier (see Figure 2-6).

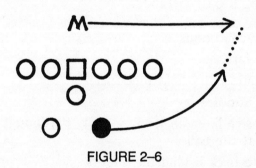

FIGURE 2–6

When pursuing (inside or outside), middle linebackers have to run as straight a course as possible. Obstacles along that course—blockers—frequently delay or eliminate the linebackers' pursuit. As encounters with blockers increase, chances of making the tackle decrease. Linebackers must quickly shed blockers in the pursuit angle. A common fault of aggressive linebackers is running off the pursuit angle to make contact with the blocker. This sidetracking delays getting to the ball.

Coaching point: Teach linebackers to run outside blocked teammates rather than inside them. (See Figure 2-7.) The inside approach delays reaching the collision point.

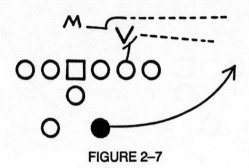

FIGURE 2–7

Pass Dropping

After the middle linebacker makes sure the play isn't a run, he has to drop for a pass. Middle backer keys for anticipating a pass include:

game conditions

long yardage

formation and field tendencies

long huddle

offensive lineman leaning back, flat-footed and cheating off the ball

quarterback licking his fingers

Quick reaction to a pass key is the first essential to a good pass drop. The pass drop should begin after the middle backer eliminates the run possibility.

As he first reacts to pass, the middle backer should focus on running backs and the quarterback for a draw key. After checking against a draw, the middle backer has to drop into his hook zone. That zone is determined by the defensive coverage. Frequently, the middle linebacker's pass responsibility is the tight-end hook zone. When responsible for this area, he should angle to drop about 10 yards into the straight-up pass pattern of the tight end (see Figure 2-8). This angle po-

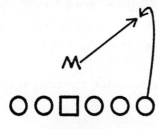

FIGURE 2–8

sitions the backer into the vision line and throwing line between the quarterback and tight end.

If the tight end runs deeper than a 10- to 12-yard hook, the middle backer should remain in that vision line between the passer and receiver. If the receiver runs a pattern deeper than the linebacker's hook zone, the backer should extend his hands and fingertips. This height barrier forces the quarterback to throw the ball higher, giving the secondary more time to react.

Coaching point: Teach the linebacker to react to where the quarterback looks and remain in the throwing line.

If the tight end runs deep through the hook zone, the middle backer should look for a receiver running underneath. If the shallow receiver tries to run a short, crossing pattern, the middle linebacker should knock him off his path before the ball is thrown—see "Rules," chapter 6.

Another common pass-drop responsibility for middle linebackers is the wide-side hook zone. If this is the side without the tight end, the middle linebacker is responsible for covering a back running a pass pattern out of the backfield. This coverage technique is covered in chapter 6.

Reading the Inside Trap

Another big-gaining play that a middle linebacker has to recognize and defend is the inside trap. To stop this play the backer must quickly recognize and react to trap keys that include:

1. Down and trap blocking scheme (see Figure 2-2B)
2. Quarterback faking an outside pitch
3. Back faking receiving a pitch and showing with open hands that he doesn't have the ball
4. Fullback or halfback running up the middle

The most recognizable trap key is the offensive guard's parallel pull and the defensive guard's unopposed penetration. The trap pull is distinguishable from the sweep pull by the guard's parallel path. (See Figure 2-9A.) The sweep pull is rounded to get depth around the corner. (See Figure 2-9B.)

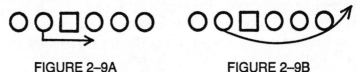

FIGURE 2–9A   FIGURE 2–9B

The inside trap is defended by the middle linebacker mirroring the trap pull. The backer's moving parallel and then stepping into the playside guard eliminates an easy angle block. (See Figure 2-10A.) When the linebacker gets outside position on the down-blocking guard, the backer can fill the trap hole. If the backer does not get outside leverage and becomes vulnerable to the angle block, he must try to drive the guard back into the trap hole (see Figure 2-10B). This action reduces the ballcarrier's maneuverability.

Your preparation for defending the inside trap includes scouting knowledge of whether your opponent has ever run

FIGURE 2–10A   FIGURE 2–10B

a "sucker trap" play (running a lone back into the hole vacated by the pulling guard). If your opponent has this play, caution your middle linebacker. But don't make your backer overcautious, because coaches are reluctant to run backs into holes blocked by "hope."

You are blessed if you have a middle linebacker who can stop the trap, reverse, and other inside runs. Your defense options increase when one strong defender can back up the middle.

3

DEVELOPING
INSIDE LINEBACKERS

An effective middle linebacker allows you options to stretch your defense into the perimeter and secondary. While two inside linebackers limit your flexibility outside and deep, the pair of inside backers strengthens your inside defense by improving your:

alignment variations
inside defensive options
stunting possibilities

At Sun Valley High School, we primarily use double inside linebacker defenses because:

1. The strength of our personnel is the linebacker-type player.

2. We specialize in running stunting defenses.

3. The strength of our opponents' offenses is the run.

4. Our defensive style has been extremely successful.

Alignments

The common defensive alignments for running two inside linebackers are the 4-4 (or split 6) and the 5-2. Double inside linebacker alignment for these defenses requires defensive designs that:

> eliminate offensive down-angles on linebackers
>
> prevent covered offensive linemen from contacting linebackers
>
> require linebackers' beating only one offensive man one-on-one

When you design even defensive fronts, the problem alignment area for inside linebackers is the uncovered tackle on the tight-end side. The linebacker on that side must align head-off the offensive tackle, eliminating the down-block (Figure 3-1).

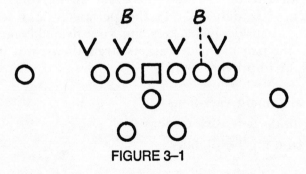

FIGURE 3–1

The split-end side linebacker in this defense can safely align off the center or stack behind either defensive lineman on his side.

The depth of the inside linebackers' alignment (discussed in relation to a middle linebacker in chapter 2) is determined by the offense you are playing and by the game situation. Also, you have the flexibility of aligning the split-side linebacker tight (1 to 1½ yards) to play run and aligning the tight-end side linebacker deeper (3 to 5 yards) to play pass. The tight and deep alignments may be interchanged if you need more pass help on the tight end.

When you loosen both linebackers in a long yardage passing situation, make sure you not only increase their depth, but also their width, giving them a start into their pass coverage areas. The additional depth also increases the linebackers' vision of the play.

Keying

While alignments for inside linebackers may vary from play to play, most keys remain regular from game to game. The standard key for a double inside linebacker is the dive back in front of him; specifically, the dive back's feet.

Drill your inside linebackers to react to their key as follows:

1. If the dive back starts a path directly toward the line, the linebacker starts a path directly toward him (see Figure 3-2A). Figure 3-2A shows a right inside linebacker reacting to a left halfback.

2. If the dive back starts a path toward the corner, the linebacker starts a scraping path to meet him (see Figure 3-2B).

3. If the dive back starts a parallel path outside, the linebacker looks to the opposite back for a trap and does not pursue outside until the ball goes outside (Figure 3-2C). Another way to recognize the trap is to look for the quarterback faking the quick pitch. Also watch for the key back with his hands extended forward, faking catching the ball, but keying he

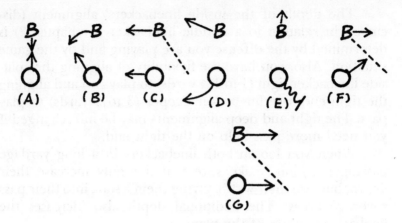

FIGURE 3–2

doesn't have the ball. (This back-out key may also be a screen pass when the back's path is combined with linemen going into the flat and the quarterback dropping extra deep.)

4. If the dive back starts a flare path into the flat, the linebacker starts dropping into his pass coverage area (Figure 3-2D).

5. If the dive back shows pass block, the linebacker also starts dropping into his pass coverage area (Figure 3-2E).

6. If the dive back starts a diagonal path inside, the linebacker looks to the other dive back and expects a crossing running play (Figure 3-2F). When backs cross (especially on the high school level) the second back usually carries the ball.

7. If the dive back starts a parallel path toward the inside, the inside backer checks the other back for a reverse and then pursues mirroring the key (Figure 3-2G).

Detailed reactions for keying dive backs in specific offenses are discussed in chapter 7.

Keying backs aligned in an "I" is similar to keying dive backs. If both backs move in the same direction, each inside linebacker should react as if the movement were that of the dive back. For example, if both "I" backs start off tackle, the onside linebacker should react similarly to his dive back heading directly toward him (meet his key back head on). The offside linebacker should react similarly to his dive back moving away from him (check reverse and then pursue).

Other specific linebacker keys for defending the "I" are discussed in chapter 7.

All dive-back reaction keys may be used with general game condition keys and should be read through an uncovered offensive lineman. A lineman showing pass, pull, or cross is an additional help to the inside linebacker.

All linebacker keys discussed indicate the initial intent of the offensive play. Variations of initial action (such as reverses, action passes, screens, and draws) must be drilled during game preparation week.

These keys have proven to be reliable through use at our school. One play that has been a problem against our keys and even-alignment has been the unexpected quarterback sneak. To defend this play, we have assigned coverage of the sneak to our right guard. ("Without our right guard, we're defenseless.") We are also teaching our linebackers to look at the quarterback until the snap.

We teach our linebackers to look at their key and at the same time see as much of the offense as possible. Vision should never be funneled to any single exclusive key.

Pursuing Inside Plays

The first area that inside linebackers should think of defending is the inside. As they look at their key backs, the linebackers should be thinking quarterback sneak, dive, trap, and inside cross.

Since their run responsibilities supersede their pass responsibilities, their first reaction steps should be forward. This forward movement prepares them against the direct inside run. The linebacker's angle for reacting to the dive is forward, through the blocker and into the dive back.

Realistically, if your linebacker stops the blocker in the neutral zone, the blocker will stop the progress of the ballcarrier. If you have a linebacker strong enough and quick enough to shed a good blocker and meet the ballcarrier at the line of scrimmage, you don't have to worry about the inside run.

While the onside backer's path is forward, the offside backer's angle is diagonal (Figure 3-3), aiming to make the tackle with his inside shoulder.

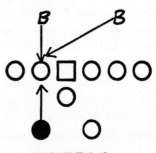

FIGURE 3–3

Ideally, inside linebackers should have the strength to make this play chest-to-chest, forcing the ballcarrier to fall backward. Most of our inside linebackers have not been strong enough to tackle high. Somehow, our smaller, quicker linebackers have learned to compensate for their size, and they defend this play adequately.

Whether your inside linebackers attack dive backs chest-to-chest or shoulder-to-thigh, they should be drilled to hit with their shoulders square and their eyes up (head up).

Squaring up the shoulders is a natural reaction for the linebacker attacking the ballcarrier headed directly toward him. A linebacker approaching from a diagonal angle, similar to the offside linebacker on a dive, has to square up unnaturally before tackling.

Pursuing Outside Plays

After first looking for inside run keys, inside linebackers must then look for outside run keys.

Techniques for inside linebackers' pursuing outside are similar to techniques for a middle linebacker's pursuing outside (discussed in chapter 2). However, there are some differences because inside linebackers are usually aligned closer to the outside than a middle linebacker. Each inside backer usually has a better view of the pulling guard key.

Good outside pursuit begins with reading and reacting to outside keys. General outside keys are discussed in chapter 2. Specific outside reaction keys for inside linebackers include:

1. The key back aligning wider and/or deeper than usual
2. A lineman pulling outside
3. The key back starting a path parallel to the line

The quickness with which an inside linebacker reacts to an outside key is determined by the scouting report and by the linebacker's responsibilities. For example, if an opponent runs a quick pitch and does not run a trap or other inside counter off the pitch, the onside linebacker can scrape outside with the key back's first outside movement.

Occasionally, when we respect a back's ability to run a quick pitch, we assign the linebacker keying him to scrape on the back's first outside movement. We play this percentage-gamble because:

1. Stopping the quick pitch is a defensive priority and we don't think we can win unless we stop that back on that play.
2. Our opponent never showed a play faking him outside and running inside.

3. Our opponent's trap play was run back to the other side where the other inside backer could cover it.

When an outside key is recognized, the inside linebackers' pursuit angles are different from the middle linebacker's pursuit angle. The onside linebacker's aim-for-collision spot should be a point about 3 yards deep on the defensive side of the line of scrimmage and about 12 yards outside the defensive end (Figure 3-4).

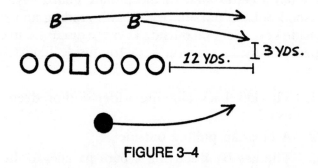

FIGURE 3–4

The offside linebacker, after checking reverse and sighting the ball and the ballcarrier running away from him, should aim for a collision point 1 yard deeper (on the defensive side) than the onside linebacker (Figure 3-4).

In almost all defensive schemes, your inside linebacker will pressure the outside play rather than contain it. When linebackers are pursuing to pressure, they should aim for the inside shoulder of the ballcarrier. This technique protects against the cutback. If your outside contain man is effective, the ballcarrier will almost always look for the cutback. Defenders pursuing outside should expect the ballcarrier to cut back.

In addition to emphasizing the cutback coaching point, you should also drill your inside backers to run initially outside with their shoulders facing the sideline, and to square up their shoulders when the ballcarrier squares up his shoulders.

Also, while pursuing, the head should be up with the eyes focused on the ballcarrier's inside shoulder. The head-up position gives the defender wider peripheral vision, enabling him to see more action. Defensive players should also learn to run without their heels contacting the ground. Running on the heels affects the vision by making a sighted object appear as if it were bouncing.

If a linebacker pursuing outside sees that his contain defender has become ineffective, the linebacker should try to stretch the play into the sideline, allowing time for inside help to get to the ballcarrier. A defender without help in this situation should avoid a quick tackling effort, because a missed tackle without nearby support could be disastrous.

Pass Dropping

Another important responsibility for inside linebackers is pass dropping into the hook zones. Similar to coaching other parts of the game, the time you allocate to coaching linebackers' pass drops should be commensurate with the time you pass drop.

Our pass-dropping practice is limited because we stunt considerably more than we pass drop. With our opponents' attacks going through a passing down cycle, we are practicing stunting more and pass dropping less.

Occasionally, one of our inside linebackers has been an exceptional pass defender; we have specialized our linebackers into a stunt linebacker and a pass linebacker. The pass-drop linebacker regularly practices pass defense with the secondary, while the run linebacker practices stunting.

Having a stunt linebacker and a drop linebacker may be a defensive key, but we play our best defensive players at what they do best. This philosophy is supported by offensive thinkers who prefer giving the ball to an outstanding running back and not using him as a decoy.

Regardless of which (or both) inside linebackers you assign to drop, his first pass reaction depends on his pass key.

General pass keys are discussed in chapter 2. Specific pass keys given by the dive back to the inside linebacker include:

> pass blocking
>
> flaring
>
> crossing flat with the other dive back
>
> poorly faking a run

Similar to run keys, dive back pass keys should be read through an uncovered lineman. Also, inside linebackers should be looking for draw keys as they read their pass keys.

The key back usually shows pass by stepping back with his outside foot and raising his arms to a pass blocking position.

A pass key off run action is the dive backs crossing before pass blocking (Figure 3-5). Crossing pass action is distinguished from crossing run action by the depth of the backs' intersection. When they cross near the line of scrimmage (usually behind the quarterback) they are keying run.

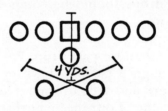

FIGURE 3–5

When the backs cross deeper (3 to 4 yards), they are keying pass. Backs cross deeper on the run fake to get better blocking angles against outside rushing defenders. That deeper angle also keys pass.

Reading the Inside Draw

As your linebackers react to their pass keys, you should train them to think and look for the inside draw.

Dive back keys that indicate draw include:

chopping the feet in place
prematurely positioning the hands to receive the ball
establishing eye contct with the quarterback
moving parallel toward the center, getting closer to the quarterback's drop path

An inside linebacker can read those dive-back keys along with these general keys for a draw:

Passing situation
Offensive linemen giving defensive linemen an easy outside pass rush route
Quarterback showing the ball high, faking a pass
Quarterback making eye contact with the draw back

As the inside linebacker reacts to a pass key and drops, he should be looking for a sign of a draw. He should continue looking for draw keys until the quarterback drops deeper than the dive backs, eliminating the threat of a hand-off.

Defending the draw is one of the responsibilities of inside linebackers. Chapter 4 discusses the responsibilities of outside linebackers.

4

COACHING OUTSIDE LINEBACKERS

All the defensive assistant coaches at Sun Valley (both of us) agree that the most difficult defensive position to play is outside linebacker (cornerback). Sun Valley corners, our most-skilled defensive athletes, have to be run pursuers and pass defenders—being tall is also helpful. Their play is critical because they are the widest aligned defensive players.

Mike Lashendock, coach at Sun Valley, has been coaching high school football for almost thirty years. He is one of the coaches who originates the ideas from which the rest of us steal. His ideas on secondary play are original, unique, and successful. His 1981 secondary was typical of Mike's success. With four of five inexperienced starters, his 1981 group:

- gave up the fewest passing yards in Delaware County (a Philadelphia suburb with thirty high schools)

- gave up one touchdown pass
- played a defense that earned 4 shutouts and gave up an average of 8.7 points per game

The following information on corner play is exclusively Mike's. It is just a sampling of his defensive knowledge. In my twenty years of listening to clinicians and talking to coaches, I've never heard a more knowledgeable defensive coach than Mike.

Alignment

Normal alignment for outside linebackers* is a yard and a half outside the tight end (wing or split-side tackle) and a yard and a half off the line of scrimmage. This distance should position the linebackers where they can't be hooked—the criteria that determine the alignment. Similar to all linebacker and secondary positioning, the depth of the alignment is altered by long yardage and game-saving situations.

Corners' normal alignment positions them to play their run and pass responsibilities. (We assign them 70 percent outside and 30 percent off tackle, and we assign our end defensive linemen 70 percent off tackle and 30 percent outside.) These responsibilities and alignment are common to outside linebacker play in 4-4 defenses.

We play a 4-4 defense—except for the corner play. Secondary coach Mike designed a unique (and proven successful) 3½-deep defense, with one standard corner. Our lone corner aligns on the tight-end side and our "half-corner" plays a walk-away alignment of the split-end side (Figure 4-1). Our tight-end side corner is our best run/pass defender and our "half-corner" is our best pass/run defender.

FIGURE 4-1

*The terms outside linebacker and cornerback are used interchangeably.

Our one corner alignment does not reduce the variations of our defensive front. We maintain the flexibility to play the philosophy of defenses such as the 4-4, 4-3, 5-2, and 6-1. For example, our "funny four" stunting defense (Figure 4-2) is a 4-2 plus one corner alignment that allow us to run the inside stunts and most outside stunts peculiar to a 4-4 defense. In addition, we have a pass defender on the side where our opponent is likely to pass.

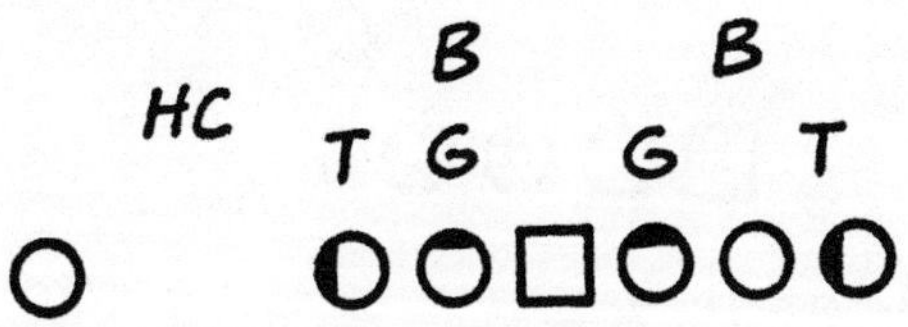

FIGURE 4–2

This alignment does not affect variations such as the 5-2. We play our 5-2 look by sliding our linemen away from the tight end (Figure 4-3). Corner play remains constant.

Our "half-corner," the better pass defender, aligns on the split-end side—where the opponent usually does more passing than running. His walk-away alignment is determined by the split-end's width. The "half-corner" is positioned to take away the quick-in and quick-out patterns.

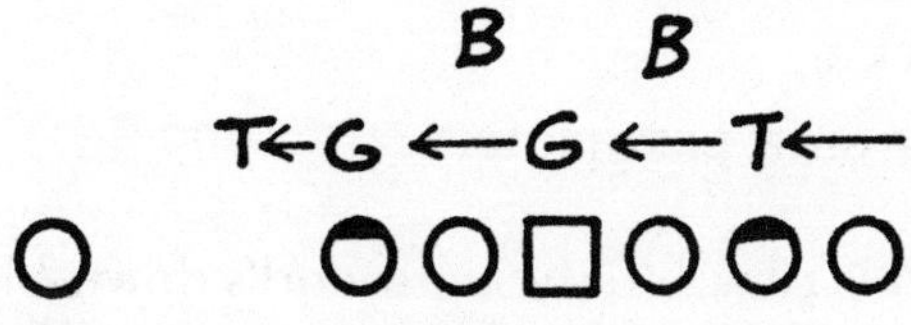

FIGURE 4–3

Keying

The keys that Mike developed for the corner include the triangle of the tight end, near back, and tackle. These outside linebacker keys can be easily adapted to your 4-4 or similar defense.

The first key to teach your corner is to look for the near dive back starting an outside quick-pitch path. Teach your corner to react to this priority key by having him turn his shoulders to face the sideline and get depth while establishing an angle of pursuit (see Figure 4-4). While reacting to this play, the corner must avoid being hooked by the tight end.

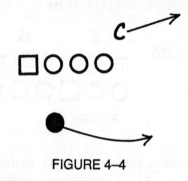

FIGURE 4–4

Reading the right end is the next important key to teach your corner. The common tight-end actions include:

blocking down on the tackle
pulling inside
blocking out on the corner
pass blocking
releasing on a pass pattern

The corner reacts to the tight-end's down-block by diagonally crossing the line of scrimmage, closing down near the original alignment position of the tight end (Figure 4-5A). After closing down, the corner should look for a pulling lineman or back trying to kick out. The corner should shed these blockers with his inside shoulder, keeping the outside shoulder free.

When closing down, the corner must avoid penetration too deeply. About 1 yard across the line of scrimmage is good depth. Deeper depths are similar to being kicked out.

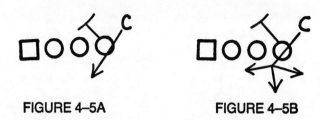

FIGURE 4–5A   FIGURE 4–5B

Option offenses may require a deeper penetration and different angles while reacting to this key (Figure 4-5B). These alternate angles are determined by which option back the corner is assigned (dive, quarterback, or pitch).

When your corner reads the tight end blocking straight out on him, teach your corner to start a collision course at the tight end. Again emphasize the coaching point of keeping the outside shoulder free.

Your corner's reaction to the tight-end pass blocking is influenced by your scouting report. If your opponent has shown a tight-end screen, condition your corner to think and look for the screen when the tight end blocks. After checking the screen, have him drop into his pass responsibility area.

Your scouting must also determine if the offensive tackle is a reliable pass key. He can help your corner read pass.

Another pass key to teach your corner is the tight end releasing on a pass pattern.

If your corner is aligned on the side of the tight end and a wing (similar to the Wing-T), he should react to the wingback similar to how he reacts to the tight end.

If you play a balanced corner defense, the split-end side corner can key the near back (through the tackle for a pass key). Reactions to the back include:

1. If the back dives ahead, close down over the tackle looking for the keep or the pitch off the dive (Figure 4-6A).

2. If the back starts parallel inside or diagonally inside, close down, look opposite, and pursue (Figure 4-6B).

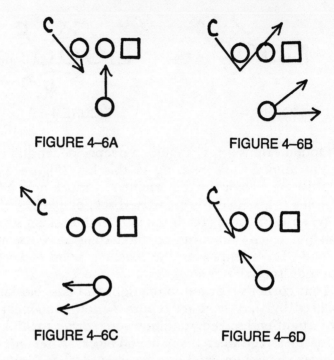

FIGURE 4–6A   FIGURE 4–6B

FIGURE 4–6C   FIGURE 4–6D

3. If the back pass blocks, drop into the pass coverage.

4. If the back starts parallel outside or flaring outside, turn the shoulders to the sideline and pursue similar to covering the quick pitch (Figure 4-6C).

5. If the dive back starts toward the corner, the corner starts a collision course toward him (Figure 4-6D).

In our "half-corner" alignment, his first priority is reading for the quick pitch, similar to the other corner. After teaching them to look for the quick pitch, Mike teaches them to read the split tackle for a pass/run key. The tackle key that he substantiates through his scouting is:

If the tackle steps forward and his head is up—react to pass.

If the tackle steps forward and his head is down—react to run.

Playing Onside Runs

When either corner reads a run coming toward him, he must play his contain position by keeping his outside shoulder free. The corner's responsibility is contain in almost all defenses.

To contain runs coming toward him, he should work to keep the ball inside him and stop the play by tackling from the outside in.

If a blocker tries to obstruct the corner, he should shed him with his inside shoulder. Two techniques for corners handling a stronger blocker:

Fake inside and step outside.

Give ground, keeping outside leverage.

A desperation technique for avoiding getting rolled over by blockers is pancaking, collapsing flat to the ground and causing the blockers to trip and pile up.

A coaching guideline for teaching corners to defend onside runs is: "Jam the power and string the sweep." When the corner closes down on the off-tackle power run, the outside break is taken away and the play is forced into the strength of the defense.

Stringing the sweep buys time for inside pursuit to catch the play. If the pursuit never arrives, a good corner will run the ballcarrier into the sideline. While stringing, the corner should maintain leverage for the cutback.

When onside runs initially develop as offside runs (reverse and bootleg), the corner should similarly try to string them out, waiting for help. Different from a sweep, a reverse or boot may necessitate the corner's dropping a few yards to maintain leverage. If inside help is unavailable, the corner should retreat until he is forced to attempt a difficult, one-on-one, open-field tackle. (Corner play versus the option is discussed in chapter 7.)

Watch for a weaker inexperienced corner being too outside conscious and containing from a location that permits a ballcarrier to run inside the corner and then get outside, outrunning the inside pursuit.

Playing Offside Runs

When a running play goes away from your corner, train him to think bootleg or some other reverse action. Coach him to react to an offside run after clearly seeing the ball crossing the line of scrimmage. Make sure his pursuit angle will position him in front of the ballcarrier (Figure 4-7). Your corner's pursuit depth should be deeper if he is slower than average.

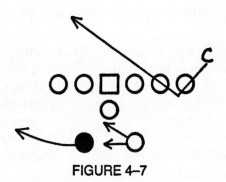

FIGURE 4–7

If the play away from the corner is a running play through the line, the corner should pursue after he clearly sees the ball pass the line of scrimmage.

Pressuring Runs

In addition to playing chasing and containing corners, you may choose to play pressure corners. When you crash your corner, have him start running on the first movement of the end or tackle.

The tackle is sometimes a better key because the rules don't permit him to reset after his hand is positioned on the ground. But if scouting shows that an opponent doesn't shift or reset the tight end, he is the better crashing key because the corner sees him better than he sees the tackle.

Thinking offensively, we use the tight end reset about once a game in a crucial situation when we need five or fewer yards. Our tight end reacts to our normal starting count by standing, taking one step outside, and then placing his hand down.

Avoiding the defensive offsides when the end moves is difficult because linemen are trained to move on movement.

Regardless of which key reaction you teach your crashing corner, he should pressure on an angle that allows him to play his responsibility. Angles and responsibilities for crashing corners include:

1. Angling to the outside shoulder of the tight end and then paralleling the offensive side of the scrimmage line to take the dive hole and also to take a down-the-line quarterback on an option play (Figure 4-8A).

2. Angling toward the outside leg of the near dive back, taking a sweep and pressuring a dropback passer (Figure 4-8B). **Coaching point:** When the crashing corner is assigned an option quarterback, the corner should try to grab three legs at the option exchange.

FIGURE 4–8A 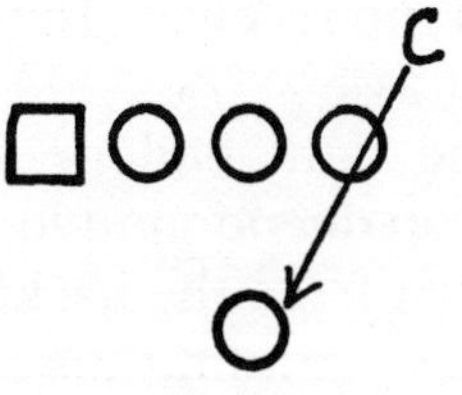   FIGURE 4–8B

3. Angling perpendicular to the line of scrimmage, taking the quarterback on some options and pressuring a roll-out passer (Figure 4-8C).

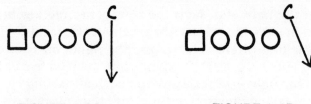

FIGURE 4–8C   FIGURE 4–8D

4. Angling into the flat, taking the pitch man on an option (Figure 4-8D).

Coaching point: This is common to all crashing angles—any contact the corner makes must be made with his inside shoulder, keeping his outside shoulder and arm free.

Pass Dropping

When a corner isn't crashing, he will have some pass responsibility. His pass drop begins when he reads a previously discussed key. He should first react to the key by back-pedaling a few steps while looking at the tight end (or wing).

Most corners are responsible for the quick out pattern. When the end starts his out break, the corner should break with him, keeping outside leverage (except into short field) until the ball is thrown. When it's thrown, the corner should front the receiver, positioning himself in the line of the ball's flight and the receiver. In this situation, a corner with height can be an asset.

If the tight end or wing doesn't release, the corner should drop deeper and look to cover a back running an outside pattern from the backfield. A middle linebacker usually covers backs running inside patterns.

If no back is out and the tight end is blocking, the corner should look toward the middle of the field for a receiver running a crossing pattern. If no receivers are running crossing patterns, the corner should work his way back toward the middle of the field.

When the "half-corner" reads a pass, teach him to drop into the path of the slant-in pattern (See Figure 4-9). This causes the receiver either to run into the defender before he catches the ball or to be hit immediately after he catches the ball. Both actions are effective.

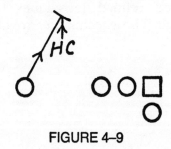

FIGURE 4–9

Reading Outside Screens

How well the corners are able to stop the outside screen depends upon their early recognition of screen keys. General indicators of a screen play include:

1. passing
2. extremely long yardage
3. play following a 15-yard penalty (high school tendency)
4. quarterback dropping extra deep
5. defensive lineman running into the flat and a back flaring with him

Teach the corners to read the tackle for a screen. You want the corner to start into the flat to break up a screen when the tackle shows his numbers toward the sideline.

This early reaction usually puts the corner behind the screen before the back catches the ball. Once there, the corner is permitted to contact the receiver behind the line of scrimmage.

Outside linebackers' early recognition of the outside screen often changes a feared offensive play into a big defensive play.

After recognizing a screen or any other play, your linebackers need refined techniques for shedding and getting to the ball. Those techniques are discussed in chapter 5.

5

SHEDDING AND GETTING TO THE BALL

Recognizing the play is a linebacker's brain work; getting to the play is his brawn work. Between recognition and the whistle, the linebacker needs an assortment of techniques that will help him shed blockers, pursue the ballcarrier, and make the tackle.

Shedding Techniques

A linebacker's best technique to meet and shed a blocker is the shoulder shed (Figure 5-1). This technique is effective because the defender can use his upper body strength and leg strength to counter the blocker's thrust. These linebacker vs. blocker encounters have a direct effect on the game's outcome. They are as important to a linebacker as the one-on-one is to a lineman.

The shoulder shed will give your linebackers an equal opportunity to defeat the blockers.

FIGURE 5–1

Coaching point: Teach the shoulder shed and other shed techniques by emphasizing that shedding is an aggressive action and not a passive method of absorbing a block. Blockers must be defeated, not just stalemated. A stalemate is an effective offensive block.

Prior to delivering the shoulder shed hit, your linebacker should widen his stance and flex his knees so that his extended down fingers can almost touch the blades of grass (or particles of dust) between his feet. This coiled-knee position supplies the leg thrust needed for the hit.

The shoulder shed is delivered by firing the upper arm and shoulder into the opponent's chest, just above the numbers.

Coaching points:

1. Thrusting off the leg on the same side as the shoulder used
2. Keeping the tail lower than the shoulders so the thrust is upward

3. Adjusting to the height of the blocker by moving the shoulder and tail as a unit, and not lowering the shoulders only

The actual shedding is the upward and outward follow-through of the forearm. This flipping action clears the blocker from the defender's pursuit path. Linebackers must master shedding with both shoulders. This skill is necessary to play aggressive defense. The better the shedder, the more effective the linebacker.

A variation of the shoulder shed is the vertical elbow lift. The shoulder, back, and foot position are the same as the shoulder shed, but the hit is delivered with the bone section of the elbow, held vertically to the ground. This technique keeps the blocker farther away from the defender, but the linebacker does not have the hitting surface that the shoulder and upper gives with the shoulder shed.

A third shedding technique that also keeps the blocker away from the linebacker's body is the forearm lift. This technique is similar to the shoulder shed and vertical lift, except that the blow is delivered with the forearm parallel to the ground.

Coaching point: Emphasize with both arm lifts, as well as with the shoulder shed, the upward and outward arm movement that clears the blocker from the pursuit path of the linebacker.

Tackling Fundamentals

Keying, reacting, shedding, and pursuing get the linebacker to the ballcarrier, but they don't make the whistle sound—and neither does a missed tackle.

Coaches like to say that many skills must be practiced every day, but if a defensive coach had time to practice only one skill daily, that skill should be tackling.

Coaching points: Teaching one set tackling form is difficult because tackling situations vary from play to play.

However, here are some points common to most tackling situations:

1. Use the sideline whenever possible.
2. Prior to contact, position the back parallel to the ground.
3. Deliver the hit with the shoulder.
4. Avoid dropping the shoulder that doesn't make contact.
5. When the shoulder hits, fully extend both arms, keeping them on the same plane and parallel to the ground (Figure 5-2).
6. Squeeze the fingers and grab some skin (or material).

FIGURE 5–2

This last point contradicts the traditional "clasp your hands." The only way tacklers can consistently "clasp their hands" is when long-arm defensive players tackle thin-waisted ballcarriers.

Assuming you don't play in that league, coach your players to squeeze their fingers and grab something when they reach around a ballcarrier and cannot find another hand.

A tackling situation that your linebackers will face infrequently is a desperation attempt to prevent a score. If your linebackers are frequently making desperate tackling attempts, stop reading and start practicing kick-off returns.

If you're still reading, two techniques are commonly used to make desperation tackles. If your linebacker is desperately chasing a ballcarrier and your player can catch him, he should jump on the ballcarrier's back, wrap his arms and legs like a spider, and lower himself until the ballcarrier is tripped.

If your linebacker can't catch the ballcarrier and can only make a desperation dive, he should dive for the ballcarrier's heel and try to slap it forward.

Another unusual tackling situation is trying to cause a fumble. A good technique for causing a fumble is to wedge the hand into the space between the ballcarrier's elbow and the back point of the ball.

Stressing Safety Techniques

Tackling techniques aren't what they used to be. Techniques you don't know and don't teach can hurt—hurt your players, hurt your pocketbook, and hurt your program. You have a responsibility to learn and teach safe techniques and to learn and discourage dangerous techniques. Also, high school coaches have been sued for teaching unsafe tackling techniques.

Sun Valley's head football coach, Bob Fithian, regularly emphasizes safety techniques in tackling by making the players and staff aware of the dangers of making contact with the top of the helmet and jamming it into ballcarriers.

This contact technique, commonly known as spearing, makes the spinal column vulnerable to serious injury.

That danger exists whenever contact is made with the head down. The neck muscles protect the neck when the head is up, not down.

Dangerous coaching practices include teaching techniques such as:

1. Putting the helmet through the football.
2. Putting the face into the ballcarrier's numbers.
3. Tackling head first.
4. Spearing by additional tacklers.

Coaches have a responsibility to actively discourage these and similar techniques.

Playing the Angles

The shortest path to pursue the ballcarrier is a straight line. Defensive football is a game of straight lines and sharp angles. Training linebackers and other defensive players to pursue in straight lines will reduce pursuit time and improve defensive statistics. If a linebacker's running path were charted during the plays of a game, the chart should contain straight lines and sharp angles.

A situation where many players misjudge the depth of an angle is when the ballcarrier is about 25 yards from the defensive player. Players in this situation underestimate the ballcarrier's speed and overestimate their own speed. The result is a pursuit angle too shallow. Angles such as these are frequently misjudged because most angle judgments are over less distance and this larger perspective is seldom calculated.

Good angles lead your linebackers to good defensive plays. When your linebackers control your opponent's running game, you can expect to see the ball in the air more. Chapter 6 will help you prepare your linebackers for pass defense.

6

PREPARING LINEBACKERS FOR PASS DEFENSE

As a general rule, your linebackers should think run first and pass second. But some situations demand your linebackers' thinking pass first and run second. The general rule can also be reversed if the defensive line can control your opponent's running game.

Whatever the situation, linebackers are an important part of your pass defense and their pass preparation should not be neglected because of their run defense priority.

This chapter will help you improve your linebackers' pass defense.

Recognizing Pass Keys

Specific pass keys for linebacker positions are discussed in previous chapters (middle linebacker, chapter 2; inside linebacker, chapter 3; and outside linebacker, chapter 4). In addition to these specific keys, a linebacker may read other pass indicators. These general observation keys (in addition to the obvious long yardage situation) include:

1. Formation key
2. Substitution key
3. Huddle key
4. Skilled-player key

A passing formation key includes not only a scouted formation tendency, but also spread and shotgun formations that isolate receivers and give them field space to run patterns.

A substitution key for pass, in addition to a better passer replacing the quarterback and a better catcher replacing a receiver, includes a passer entering the game at a position where he can throw a halfback pass or a double pass. Another similar key is a specialized receiver entering at split-side setback, a position where he can run a combination pattern with the split receiver. A back positioned here has quick access to running a pattern out of the backfield.

Also, long huddles generally indicate pass because passing terminology usually requires more explanation than running terminology. Another possible huddle key is oral or visual communication between a quarterback and a receiver.

An offensive lineman keys the pass by trying to get an alignment advantage before setting up for pass blocking. He may align off the ball or take a stance with his heels, head, and tail leaning backward, trying to get a backward advantage off the ball.

A quarterback occasionally keys pass by communicating with a receiver during the approach to the ball. Walking to the line, he may lick his fingers, or look at a receiver, or at a defensive back during cadence. The quarterback should be observed for patterned mannerisms common to pass plays.

Wide receivers should also be observed for similar pass play mannerisms which could include:

1. A faster approach from the huddle to the ball
2. A different facial expression
3. A hand mannerism (licking, wiping, stretching)
4. Staring at a defender in the area of the pattern

Studying the offense for a pass key is like trying to steal signs from a coach or player in baseball. Knowing any sign that keys a pass play can make playing pass defense a little easier.

Reacting to Action Passes

After learning such sophisticated keys for a pass play, your linebackers will still have a problem recognizing action passes. When your opponent runs well, your linebackers will react to signs of run. Learning to react to a pass off a run is a problem, especially learning to react to an action pass in a run situation.

The first key to defending an action pass is a situation key. In a passing situation, your linebackers should think exclusively pass. Initial run action should be disregarded because the long yardage offers a cushion for slowly reacting to a run.

A recognizable action pass key for linebackers is a poor run fake by an offensive back, which includes:

1. Running to the line at a slower speed
2. Running straight up rather than bent over
3. Positioning the hands poorly during the fake
4. Discontinuing the fake before running into the line

Your linebackers can also read an action pass from the offensive linemen. Since these linemen aren't permitted downfield on a pass, they often key the action pass by showing a one-step aggressive fire-out block and then straightening up.

Reacting to the Ball

Early reaction to a pass key gives your linebacker a quick start into his pass coverage area. His initial drop step should start the angle that will position him in his primary pass responsibility area; flat, curl, hook, etc. That linebacker angle should vary from game to game, depending on the opponent's short passing tendencies.

Whatever the linebacker's drop angle, he should check for a draw, screen, and trick play during the first few drop steps. After that, the linebacker should look into the quarterback's eyes to read any adjustments to the originally planned angle. Most quarterbacks cannot "look off" a defender. If the passer has the ability to look one way and then pick up another receiver, you have to prepare your linebackers accordingly. If the quarterback looks only to the receiver he is throwing to, train your linebackers to react to where he looks.

The eye key will lead the linebacker to the general location where the ball is being thrown. The specific location is keyed when the passer raises his front (nonthrowing side) shoulder. Raising the lead shoulder is generally the point of no return for the passer. The raised shoulder is the linebacker's key to run to the ball.

Going for the ball or going for the receiver is determined by your philosophy and the game situation. You would like the interception, but are you willing to sacrifice the consequences of a missed tackle in the secondary?

Coaching point: When playing the receiver and the ball, teach going for the ball (at the highest point) with the inside hand, and going for the tackle with the outside hand.

Covering Backs in Pass Patterns

A linebacker's pass responsibility is usually covering a short hook zone or a short curl zone. Frequently, he must cover a back man-for-man. Coaches like to design pass patterns that require linebackers to cover backs because the back usually has more maneuverability than the linebacker.

For your linebackers to cover that back, you have to emphasize early pass recognition, flawless technique, and a good rush up front.

Your linebacker's normal pass keys will give him the early recognition. In addition, your linebacker may observe a back's individual key such as his aligning a step closer or wider.

A linebacker's technique for covering a back is to keep in front of the back by about 5 yards and to take away the inside cuts. At all times during the coverage, the linebacker must have an awareness of the passer and the receiver. Mike uses the expression "one eye and one eye," one eye on the passer and one eye on the receiver.

The philosophy behind taking away the inside patterns is that forcing an outside pattern requires a longer pass. This gives the linebacker more reaction time. Also, a linebacker can cover an out pattern by positioning himself in the throwing lane between the passer and the receiver (Figure 6-1).

If a back beats your linebacker, teach him to turn his back and sprint toward the receiver. If your linebacker

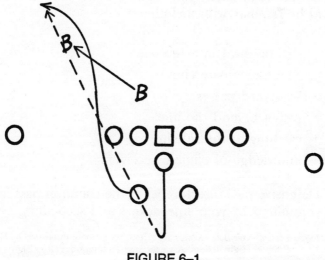

FIGURE 6–1

catches up to the receiver, his last resort is running through the receiver's hands when the ball touches them. If your linebacker doesn't catch up to the receiver, start thinking about your PAT (Points After Touchdown) defense.

Knowing Pass Defense Rules

Teaching rules related to pass defense should be an important part of your linebacker and secondary preparation. Rules will not only make your linebackers aware of what they can't do, but they will also make them aware of what they can do. For example, your linebackers should know that if a defensive lineman tips a forward pass, defensive players are permitted to make contact with receivers before the offense has an opportunity to catch the ball.

Most pass defense rules have remained constant in recent years, but as a conscientious coach, you should study current rule changes that are listed in front of each year's new rule book.

The rules discussed in this book are from the *National Federation of State High School Associations.**

Other Federation pass-related rules that linebackers should be familiar with include:

- definition of interference
- simultaneous catches
- backward passes
- passes behind the line
- catching at the sideline
- knowledge of eligible receivers

Defensive pass interference is the common pass infraction committed by your linebackers and secondary. Gener-

*1982 Football Rule Book, National Federation Edition. Published by National Federation of State High School Associations, Federation Place, Elgin, Illinois 61020.

ally, defenders are not permitted to make contact with receivers until the offense has the opportunity to catch the ball. The National Federation rule (Article 6a) says: "It is interference: a. If any player of A or B (offense or defense) who is beyond the neutral zone, interferes with an eligible opponent's opportunity to move toward, catch, or bat the ball, except that it is not interference if unavoidable contact occurs when two or more eligibles are making a simultaneous and bona fide attempt to move toward, catch, or bat the ball."

The part of this rule that allows your linebackers and secondary to play aggressive pass defense is ". . . if unavoidable contact occurs. . . ." The "unavoidable contact" is an official's opinion and coaches and officials don't share similar opinions.

A judgment that coaches and officials agree on more often is a simultaneous catch. Your defenders should know that when the offense and defense catch the ball simultaneously, the offense maintains possession. Aggressive pass defense must include catching the ball exclusively or not allowing the offense to catch it.

Another rule that your linebackers should know is that an incompleted backward pass is a live ball and may be advanced. (College rules permit only the recovery and not the advancement.) Your players can be alerted to the incompleted backward pass by the absence of a whistle when the ball hits the ground. Backward passes frequently occur when a screen or flare pattern is forced deeper than usual.

Another pass rule related to screens and flares is that a linebacker cannot commit pass interference while defending these plays behind the line of scrimmage. Your linebackers are permitted to go aggressively through these behind-the-line receivers to get to the ball.

Linebackers should also know the rule for making a legal catch on the sideline. This rule gives receivers approximately 1 additional yard to catch the ball over the boundary line. Only one foot (or any other part of the body) has to be touching inbounds when making a catch on the sidelines.

The one foot inbounds rule means playing receivers tighter on the sidelines than if two feet had to be touching inbounds.

Another rule that linebackers should know is the identification of eligible receivers. Offensive players permitted to catch the ball are players on each end of the line and the four offensive backs, if they align a yard or more into the backfield. In 1980, the National Federation mandated that an eligible receiver must wear an eligible pass receiver number (1 to 49, 80 to 89). Any numbered player may align at a pass receiving position, but only an eligible-numbered player may run downfield on a pass play.

Recognizing eligible receivers usually isn't a problem for your linebackers, but your teaching of rules should include showing your linebackers, and secondary, unusual formations and pass plays that have been used by your opponents or by other teams in your area.

We familiarize our pass defenders with:

- Throwback to the quarterback off a sweep (Figure 6-2)

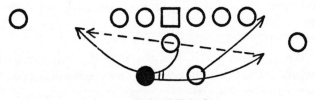

FIGURE 6–2

- Additional pass off the above throwback
- Center being an eligible receiver on the end of the line (Figure 6-3)
- Crossfield backward pass on the kick off
- Double passes
- Underhand thrown forward passes (usually thrown behind the line)
- Stop passes and a pitch back to a trailer

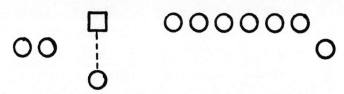

FIGURE 6–3

Knowing unusual pass plays and pass related rules will help your linebackers to be fully prepared to defend the pass. Previous chapters helped you prepare linebackers for the running game.

Chapter 7 combines pass and run preparation and helps you prepare your linebackers against specific offenses (Veer, Pro, Wing T, and goal line).

7

LINEBACKER PLAY VS. SPECIFIC OFFENSES

The purpose of drilling and skilling your linebackers is to stop your opponent's offense on game day. Your general preparation to stop a specific offense is a year-round job. You can learn the strengths and weaknesses of offenses you play against by going to clinics, talking to other coaches, studying films, and reading books, articles, and play manuals. After you understand the philosophy and objectives of an offense, you can then start to prepare the specific variations and adaptations that your opponent runs. This means that the basic principles of defending the Veer don't change from opponent to opponent, but preparation to compensate for the plays they run well and don't run well will change.

Linebacker Play Vs. the Veer

The Veer is difficult to defend because it can adjust in progress to attack weak defensive areas. The defensive problem is determining where to make your defense strongest (inside, outside, or off tackle). The defensive position that does the most adjusting to the Veer's strengths and weaknesses is the linebackers.

Specific linebacker problems for defending the Veer include:

1. What areas do you defend strongest and weakest? (If you play a balanced defense, you are mismatched where your opponent is strongest.)

2. What tendencies do they have for running: the give, the keep, the pitch, counters, and pass?

3. What plays do they run off their basic option?

4. When and where do you have to play more than man-to-man on the dive, keep, and pitch?

5. How do you adjust to strong and weak formation sides?

6. How do you gamble linebacker coverage?

7. What linebacker keys are available?

Your scouting report has to give you specific answers to these questions. To analyze adequately your opponent's Veer tendencies, you have to scout by charting the following:

- situations
- field positions
- formations
- plays

This information will give you specific intricacies of your opponent's Veer offense (or any other offense). You will know:

- The plays they run and how often they run each one
- The down, distance, and field position characteristic of each play

Over the past few years, our Veer opponents have shown the following tendencies:

- Dive on first and ten
- Counter option or reverse on third and long
- Quarterback keep or pitch on long yardage
- Dive to the tight-end side more than the split-end side
- Favorite back that usually runs the dive
- Favorite back that usually gets the pitch
- Quarterback that is usually a strong runner

Your analysis will give you specifics for playing your Veer opponent, but some general principles are applicable for almost every Veer offense. You can defend a strong inside Veer team by playing two linebackers between the tackles (standard 5-2 and 4-4). In these defensive alignments, each linebacker can key a dive back and play that back man-to-man. This alignment also gives you options to strengthen your defense against a specific Veer team:

1. You can play your best linebacker on their best back.
2. You can play your best linebacker on the wide side.
3. You can play your best linebacker on the strong side.

Inside linebackers' alignment should not give an uncovered lineman an angle block, giving the offense a dive hole. Inside backers should align in a stack or head off an uncovered lineman (Figure 7-1). These backers should key the feet of the near dive back. Feet are usually the earliest indication of movement. Inside backers must learn the following reactions to their key back's feet:

- If the feet go straight to the line, as on a dive play, the linebacker has to meet him head on, making the

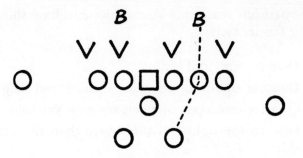

FIGURE 7–1

hit with the inside shoulder. (The outside shoulder is kept free to pursue outside on a fake dive and pitch.)

If the feet go away parallel to the line, the linebacker has to take an angle of pursuit across the field (Figure 7-2). The linebacker starts this angle when the back takes his third parallel step. This delay eliminates the chances of the key back turning around and running the counter option (Figure 7-3).

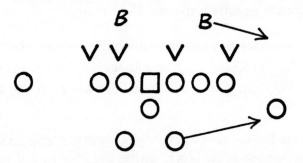

FIGURE 7–2

These keys are the common movements of backs in the Veer offense. If your opponent combines a Pro offense with the Veer, you can teach your linebackers those keys as well as the Veer keys. (Pro formation keys are explained later.)

In addition to the feet key, inside linebackers should react to a quarterback's specific movement on option plays.

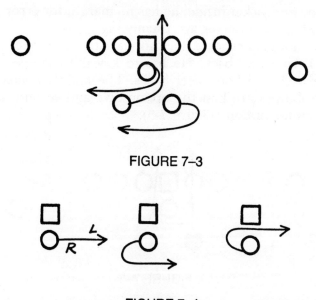

FIGURE 7–3

FIGURE 7–4

Common quarterback option movements include an open step, a reverse pivot, or a counter option pivot (Figure 7-4) before moving down the line on the dive. This information comes from scouting.

The quarterback movement and the back's feet give your inside linebackers keys for defending the option-give, keep, and pitch. These keys give you strong man-to-man coverage on the dive backs.

When the inside linebacker reads his back diving, he should attack him with his inside shoulder, keeping the outside shoulder free to pursue outside if the dive is a fake. Many backs give early indications that they are not getting the dive by showing these movements:

- Wrapping the upper body around the ball when the fake hand-off is being made
- Straightening up as soon as the fake is made

When two linebackers are playing inside, each linebacker has a backup on the inside dive play. When you play one linebacker inside, he has no margin for error. Middle linebacker mistakes are usually big gains.

A middle linebacker does not have the security of exclusively keying one back. He has to key the triangle of the quarterback and both Veer backs. The middle linebacker's responsibilities are first the option-dive and second the inside counter option (Figure 7-5).

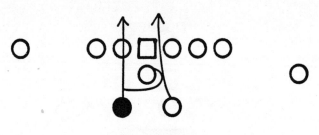

FIGURE 7–5

In addition to reading the triangle and stopping the dive and counterdive, the middle linebacker has to beat the block of the center. The middle backer's difficult responsibilities can be made somewhat easier if he aligns 2½ to 3 yards off the ball. This extra depth gives him several advantages:

1. It gives him better vision of his triangle key.
2. It allows him to attack the dive back from an outside-in angle (Figure 7-6).

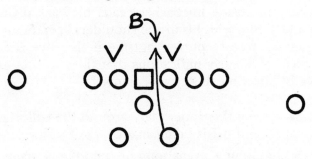

FIGURE 7–6

3. It decreases his chances of getting screened by an offensive lineman's block on a defensive lineman.

4. It allows recovery time to react to the counterdive.

5. It helps outside pursuit.

Playing one linebacker in the middle gives you the option of playing another inside linebacker on the tight-end side of the offensive formation. This alignment with the "extra" linebacker gives you an opportunity to run a variety of man-to-man coverage stunts to defend the option (Figure 7-7).

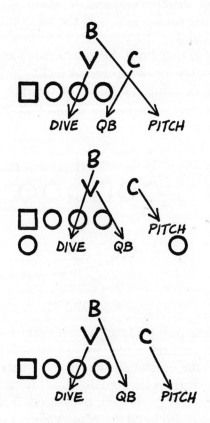

FIGURE 7–7

Each stunt gives you man-to-man coverage with a selection of attacking patterns. You have different attack angles for pressuring the dive back, quarterback, and pitch back. These stunt combinations, involving your corner, outside down lineman, and inside linebacker can be run on the strong side of the offensive formation or on the wide side of the field. They are aimed at attacking the option at the critical points where the ball is being exchanged.

When you use linebackers to strengthen your defense on one side, you are usually weaker on the other side, but your defense matches your opponent, strength against strength and weakness against weakness.

When the option is run to the weak side (the side without the tight end or the short hash-mark side), your weakside linebacker can play both the quarterback and the pitch back by using a delaying stringing-out technique. This technique is played by delaying the tackle of the quarterback, making him run parallel to the line of scrimmage as long as possible (Figure 7-8).

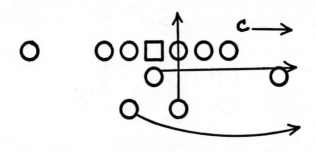

FIGURE 7–8

Coaching point: Have the defender extend his arm toward the pitch back when using the string-out technique. This creates the optical illusion that the defender is closer to the pitch back than he actually is. This causes the quarterback to think the pitch back is covered. The extended arm technique was initiated at Sun Valley by our secondary coach, Mike Lashendock, after watching baseball players taking a lead off first base with an arm extended back toward the bag, giving the illusion of being closer than they actually are.

This string-out technique with the extended arm is good for linebackers or corners when they are in a position where they have to defend both the quarterback and the pitch back.

Outside linebackers (corners) have a difficult assignment playing the option because they have to play two or three backs in an area extending from the hash mark to the sideline (or wider).

Many standard defenses dictate the corner playing the pitch back. One effective technique is to attack the pitch back as quickly as possible, before he can get started with the ball. The corner should attach high and from the outside-in. This approach forces the back to the inside if the tackle is missed or broken. The high tackle jars the back's arms either before he catches the pitch or immediately after he catches the ball. Contact at either time increases the danger of the pitch.

Good linebacker play is the key to defending any offense, but especially the Veer because it can quickly attack inside, off tackle, or outside. To be effective against this offense, linebackers have to key their back, react, look for alternate keys, and react again. This is a difficult challenge—but linebackers like challenges.

You can reduce strategically your linebackers' difficulty of playing the option by varying option assignments and techniques. For example, don't give the quarterback the comfort of knowing which defender is assigned to him or how (aggressive or passive) that defender will be playing him.

We like to start defending an option opponent by having our corner crash down aggressively on the quarterback, while our defensive tackle (defensive end) slants outside to cover the pitch back. (Our inside linebacker takes the dive.) This early aggressive technique on the quarterback usually makes him anticipate being hit the remainder of the game.

Our end lineman and cornerback interchange assignments throughout the game, but in a definite passing situation we like to have our corner assigned to the pitch back. From this coverage we can better defend the pass (with our corner playing his regular responsibility) if the offense doesn't run the option. If our lineman were assigned the pitch man, he (our lineman) would have to assume the crashing corner's normal pass responsibility.

We vary our option coverage inside by stunting one of our inside linebackers and filling every gap.

This kind of stunt and other variations will help reduce the effectiveness of your opponent's option attack.

Linebacker Play Vs. the Wing T

Linebackers playing against the option have the problem of stopping a high-gambling offense that changes as plays develop. In contrast to the Veer, the Wing T is a more conservative offense and it has stronger tendencies than the option, but it isn't any easier to defend.

Before a linebacker can effectively stop the Wing T, he must become familiar with characteristics of that offense:

1. Plays are run in sequence with a variety of plays starting with the same basic action.
2. The favorite outside play is the sweep.
3. A double-team block usually occurs at the point of attack.
4. Pulling lineman usually key the point of attack.
5. Misdirection usually precedes the play direction.

Similar to defending the option, linebackers have to recognize play patterns as quickly as possible. This requires knowing the opponent's tendencies within the Wing T offense.

The University of Delaware's Wing T is a complicated offense that contains a few basic plays and numerous sequential plays off those basic plays. Many high school coaches, and some college coaches, don't use the complete Delaware offense, but adapt parts of it to their personal needs and preferences. Because of these adaptations, most coaches have strong Wing T tendencies that were not meant to be part of the University of Delaware's offense.

A Wing T offense that our school regularly plays has the following tendencies:

- Sweep to the wing side
- Bootleg to the short side
- Fullback trap on first down and on short yardage
- Pass primarily in a passing situation
- Quick pitch to the short side of the field
- Wingback scissors to the short side of the field

Our opponents who have run the Wing T have very few basic plays and very few variations, but they run those limited plays extremely well. The defense knows the keys, knows the basic play action and the variation plays, but stopping them is still a problem.

Almost all Wing T opponents will have the inside fullback trap. To defend it, your linebackers have to know:

1. The down, distance, and field position they like to run.
2. The blocking scheme.
3. The variation plays off the trap (bootleg, pass, and so forth).

The keys to stopping the trap and other Wing T plays are not as simple as the keys for the Veer. To stop the trap, the inside linebacker has to key the trap guard and the middle blocking pattern. On the high school level, pulling linemen are strong keys for the Wing T trap and other offensive plays. This key is good because linemen pull on almost every play. Coaches are not likely to run a sucker trap play (Figure 7-9) where a guard pulls falsely and the back runs through

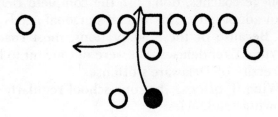

FIGURE 7–9

the hole that the coach hopes was vacated by the defensive lineman and linebacker.

Most high school coaches don't have the backfield depth to run this play regularly, because if the defense isn't fooled, the back runs into an unblocked hole. We play approximately two Wing T teams each season. Over the past eighteen seasons, we have never been hurt by the sucker trap play—that's why we key guards and other pulling linemen against the Wing T.

If you prefer a more conservative linebacker key against the Wing T, you could teach keying a combination of a pulling lineman with a back moving in the same direction.

When an inside linebacker reads a key indicating trap action, he has to meet the blocker head on and close down the distance between himself and the blocker. Closing down on the blocker closes the hole, limiting the fullback's space to break off the block (Figure 7-10). If the linebacker gives

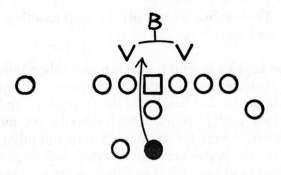

FIGURE 7–10

ground, he is opening the size of the hole for the back to run through. The larger the hole, the more difficult it will be for the inside pursuit to stop the play.

While the trap is the big inside play for the linebacker to stop, the sweep is the big outside play for him to stop. The first difficulty in stopping the sweep is that it begins to develop like the inside trap (Figure 7-11). The key for reading the sweep is again the guards. One or both guards usually pull in the direction of the sweep.

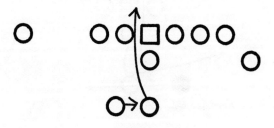

FIGURE 7–11

In addition to the guards keying the sweep, a down block or double team by the wing indicates the play. Other play action on the sweep includes:

- The fullback diving to fill for one of the pulling guards
- The quarterback going straight back and handing the ball to the halfback

When an inside linebacker recognizes this sweep action, and when he's sure the quarterback has not been fooled, he should start an angle of pursuit to the corner. While pursuing, he should follow the inside shoulder of the ballcarrier, avoiding overrunning the cutback. Approaching the corner, he should try to use the offensive double-team as a screen to hide from the ballcarrier.

Thorough scouting and film study can give you additional keys for playing the sweep. Our scouting indicated

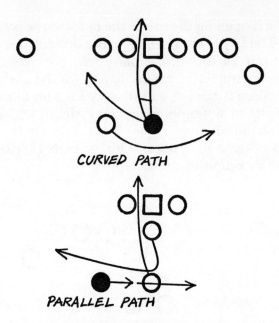

FIGURE 7–12

that an opponent showed us when they were running the trap and when they were running the sweep. On the trap, the halfback would take a path away from the line of scrimmage; on the sweep, he would take a path parallel to the line of scrimmage (Figure 7-12). Keys of this type are characteristic of a particular back. By carefully observing the movements of individual backs, especially high school backs, you can pick up additional keys for the Wing T and any other offense. All this can reduce the difficulty of the linebacker's job.

Linebacker Play Vs. the Pro

Playing linebacker against the Pro offense is not as difficult as playing against the Wing T, but mistakes can be just as costly. Playing against the Pro is easier than playing against some other offenses because keys are more consistent and the variations of basic plays are limited.

Similar to the Veer, the linebacker's key for defending the Pro is the back's feet. They are good keys to the basic running plays of a Pro (dives, sweeps, off tackle, counters, quick pitch, and trap). Also, since the Pro is primarily a passing offense, linebackers almost always have to expect a screen, draw, and bootleg. These three plays initially develop as other plays, but an alert linebacker can easily recognize variations that key the play. (Keys for recognizing these special plays are discussed in chapter 4.)

Against a standard Pro offense, the linebacker should key the feet of the nearest back in the backfield (excluding wings and slots). Standard 4-4 and 5-2 defenses have a linebacker on each side to key the back on their side. The standard 4-3 defense has a middle linebacker to key one back and an outside linebacker to key the other back.

If you use two inside linebackers, their alignment varies from head off an uncovered offensive tackle to a stack behind the inside defensive lineman. The inside linebacker on the offensive tight-end side has to play head off the offensive tackle so that he doesn't give that tackle an angle block on the dive, off tackle, or sweep.

On the offensive split-end side, the inside linebacker can stack behind the inside down lineman because the offensive tackle on that side is covered by a defensive lineman, eliminating his coming down on the linebacker.

After inside linebackers are properly aligned, they should react to their key as follows:

- If the key takes a diagonal course inside, the linebacker looks for another back to cross behind the key back (Figure 7-13).
- If the key moves away from him on a course parallel to the line, the linebacker checks to see if the other set back is moving in the same direction. If he is, the linebacker takes a straight path to the ballcarrier (Figure 7-14).
- If the key back pass blocks, the linebacker checks

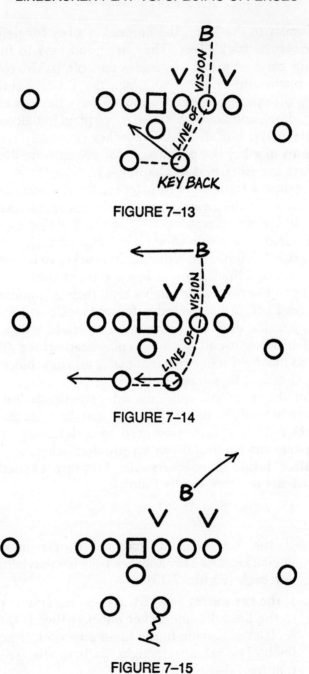

FIGURE 7–13

FIGURE 7–14

FIGURE 7–15

draw and screen, and then takes a crossover step and sprints back to his hook zone (Figure 7-15).

- If the key back moves parallel away from the linebacker, he looks inside for the other back to run inside on a trap. The linebacker does not pursue outside until he sees the ball go out.
- If the key back takes a path directly toward the offensive end, the linebacker takes a straight path to meet him.

Pro backs in an I alignment are a little more difficult to key, but that difficulty is offset by the inability of the I backs to get outside quickly (as with the quick pitch). Inside linebackers key I backs by reading the first back that comes to their side.

Since the I formation usually specializes with a good blocker leading a good ballcarrier, the strength of an I play is the runner following the blocker. Consequently, linebackers can key both I backs together. When both do not run together, either the ballcarrier runs without his lead blocker or the second-best ballcarrier gets the ball.

However, linebackers can use an additional key to read deceptive plays from the I. When backs cross on the high school level, the second back almost always gets the ball. If you find this tendency in your scouting, your linebackers will have an advantage knowing that the first back to cross has never previously carried the ball.

In the Pro I formation and in the other Pro backfield formations, linebackers should also key their backs by looking through uncovered linemen. An uncovered lineman can easily key pass, trap, sweep, etc. The uncovered lineman key, with the back key, gives linebackers early indications of where the Pro offense is attacking.

Outside linebackers (4-4 corner backs) can also key a Pro offense by reading the near back. The corners' reactions to the back key are as follows:

1. If the key back heads straight at the corner, he has to meet him on a collision course (Figure 7-16).

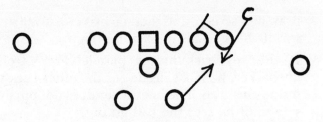

FIGURE 7–16

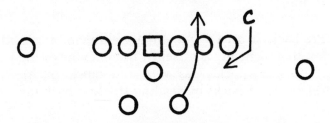

FIGURE 7–17

2. If the key back dives, the corner plays run by coming across the line of scrimmage, looking for the option or pitch off the dive (Figure 7-17).

3. If the key back goes opposite, the corner looks for flow coming back. If no action is coming back, he drops two steps, still looking for a bootleg or reverse, and then pursues through the secondary (Figure 7-18).

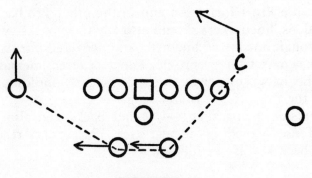

FIGURE 7–18

4. If the key shows pass, the corner drops into his pass responsibility area.

5. If the key back flares into the flat, the corner drops off the line into the flat (Figure 7-19).

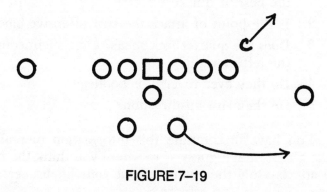

FIGURE 7–19

The keys for outside and inside linebackers will give your defense early recognition to the plays of a Pro offense. This early recognition for linebackers is important so that potentially big plays are stopped before they can get started.

Linebacker Play Vs. Goal-Line Offenses

Playing against your opponent's goal-line offense requires specific linebacker strategies that aren't used in any other field position. To defend the goal line successfully, you need a perfect defensive game plan, perfect execution, and luck.

To design a goal-line game plan for your linebackers, you have to scout the following information concerning your opponent's tendencies inside the ten and inside the five:

• down and distance tendencies
• formation tendencies
• play tendencies
• hash-mark tendencies

Look for goal-line tendencies such as:

1. Does a favorite back carry the ball? (Usually this will be the most powerful running back—not necessarily the best or quickest back.)
2. Is the point of attack the best offensive blocker?
3. Does the quarterback sneak? On a silent count? To the left or right?
4. Do they ever reverse or bootleg?
5. Do they run misdirection?

You have to compute this information mentally and make a percentage guess as to where you think the offense will attack. Only then can you put your linebackers in the best position to stop a score.

In our goal-line defense, we like to have a lineman in every offensive gap and a middle linebacker who is free to look for specific goal-line plays.

Whenever you align your linebackers on the goal line, they have to concentrate on keeping the ball (not necessarily the ballcarrier) out of the end zone. To do this, linebackers have to attack the ballcarrier on a north and south angle. A good tackling technique for linebackers in this situation is to drive a shoulder through the ball, forcing the ballcarrier to fall backward rather than forward.

Good linebacker play against the goal line and other specific offenses demands knowing the offense, reading the keys, and reacting to the play.

8

STUNTING LINEBACKERS

If your style of defense is to attack and make something happen, the stunting game is your best friend. A stunting defense continuously pressures your opponent. It's similar to full-court press in basketball and a running game in baseball.

Much of our defensive success is because we avoid playing linemen one-on-one. Our small quick guards (interior defensive linemen) traditionally have been effective slanting and playing gaps, but traditionally ineffective playing head up. This philosophy has equalized us against stronger offensive guards, and it negates offensive guards doing what they do best, blocking one-on-one.

Our slanting guards have been backed by strong linebackers who are able to cover the areas away from where the defensive .linemen slant. Occasionally, the linebackers check those uncovered gaps, but frequently they stunt through them.

Stunting linebackers force your opponent into thinking of picking up the blitz and playing audible away from the pressure. These results alone will help your defense, in addition to the actual stunt. The constant threat of blitzes forces the offense into thinking defensively before they think offensively.

We have been stunting linebackers successfully for ten years. When our opponents prepare for us, they make adjustments to their offense by practicing cutting off our stunts and attacking away from our stunting linebacker. Our opponents usually tighten their line splits and prepare their interior linemen to block two linebackers coming up the middle.

Using toe-to-toe offensive linemen almost eliminates our stunting, but it also reduces the width of the offensive area we have to defend. When tight lines have eliminated shooting linebackers through, we have had success aligning defensive linemen in gaps and charging from a goal-line technique. When we can't stunt through a line or split a seam, we usually lose.

Part of the effectiveness of our stunting is that our opponents expect a stunt every play. Our opponents' play calling includes thinking about stopping our stunting. This causes offensive linemen to think about where the defense is attacking and reduces their thinking about where the offense is attacking.

Playing the Percentages

Successful stunting necessitates having a repertoire of stunts that allows you to attack at the ideal location, regardless of the formation. Also, a stunting defense is not synonymous with a gambling defense. You can stunt linebackers and also safely defend other defensive areas. Also, you can intelligently gamble safely by stunting a linebacker into the opponents' strongest area, while weakening your coverage in your opponents' weakest area.

For example, if your opponent generally doesn't throw

short to the tight-end, you don't have to cover that short area with the same coverage that you would if they did throw short. Your linebacker assigned to that short zone would be an excellent linebacker to stunt. In essence, you are stunting a linebacker into your opponent's strength, while weakening your coverage from your opponent's weakness—the odds of success are much better than your chances of success at the casino.

When our opponent has successfully completed a tight-end pass in a zone vacated by a linebacker, we have learned (from game experience) not to panic and not to avoid that stunt. Most offensive play callers lack the patience to repeatedly throw to the tight end. A high school team seldom consecutively runs the same play the length of the field. Even more rarely does a high school team consecutively run the same pass play the length of the field.

High school teams are reluctant to pass the length of the field because the pass can be stopped by the

1. Quarterback throwing inaccurately
2. Receiver missing a catchable pass
3. Catch lacking first down yardage
4. Offensive lineman not picking up the stunt
5. Offensive lineman not preventing a defensive lineman from deflecting the ball

These offensive breakdowns are realistic (especially on the high school level) and they increase the percentage of successfully giving up a passing zone to stunt.

To stunt where your opponents are strong and slack where they aren't, you first have to study their strengths and weaknesses, and second, you need a flexible stunting attack.

If you communicate defensive signs from the sideline you must be able to signal blitzes that capitalize on your opponent's weaknesses. For example, if your opponent has a strong tendency to run to the tight-end side, you have to be able to stunt into that area (if you choose), regardless of the side the tight-end aligns. Calling a stunt right or left does not always blitz your linebacker on the tight-end side.

Other situations also dictate your calling a right or left blitz. For example, if you want to stunt a linebacker into the wide side of the field or from the left side because the quarterback is right-handed and likes to roll right, you need a left call.

To have the flexibility to make a percentage gamble and to be able to stunt according to the offense's tendencies, your defensive signal calling must include communication that allows you to blitz linebackers as follows:

- tight-end side or split-end side
- right side or left side
- wide field side or short field side
- weak-formation side or strong-formation side

We use our tight-end side and split-end side calls when we are playing an opponent that has a tendency to run to the tight end and pass to the split end. These options allow us to stunt an inside linebacker to the tight-end side in a run situation and away from the split-end side in a passing situation. This gives us a pass dropping linebacker where they like to throw and a blitzing linebacker where they don't usually throw.

We use our right side and left side calls when we want to stunt a linebacker on the short side of the field and drop a linebacker on the wide side.

We utilize the latter two options by a "slide" call or a "puppy" call. (We say "puppy" because we don't play ferociously enough to be called a monster.) From our standard two-inside linebacker defense, "puppy" means that the assigned blitzing linebacker crashes from the strong side of the opponent's formation (Figure 8-1). The strong side is determined from scouting. The strong side may be the:

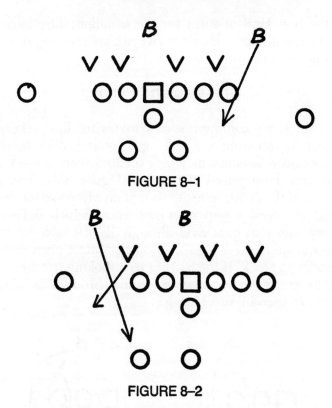

FIGURE 8–1

FIGURE 8–2

- side of the lone dive back (Figure 8-2)
- slot side
- wing side
- better or best running back side
- tight-end side

We like to stunt an inside linebacker into our opponent's strong-side run tendency and keep home our other inside linebacker to scrape.

These communications dictate the alignment of the blitzing linebacker. After the alignment is called, you have to call the best kind of stunt for the situation. The most common kinds of strongside stunts we use are crossing stunts and picking stunts.

Crossing and Picking

The most common stunts involving linebackers and linemen are crossing and picking. Crossing action between a backer and a lineman may be executed from a stack alignment and a staggered alignment (Figure 8-3). The effectiveness of the crossing action is that an offensive lineman assigned to block a gap does not know which defender is coming into that gap. Even though an offensive lineman is taught to step into that gap, at some point he must look for a defender to block. If the blocker isn't looking for the stunt or if he looks for the wrong man coming through, the stunt has a good chance of succeeding.

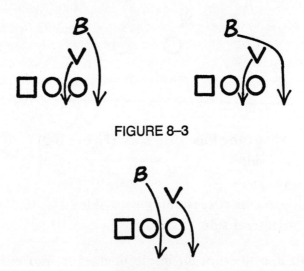

FIGURE 8–3

FIGURE 8–4

Without crossing action between the linebacker and defense linemen, the offensive linemen have clear vision of the stunt (Figure 8-4) and noncrossing action usually isn't as effective.

Our favorite crossing stunts involve inside linebackers and guards. From an even defensive alignment, the guards cross and the linebackers blitz (Figure 8-5).

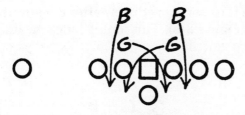

FIGURE 8–5

Coaching point: Be sure that the defensive lineman and linebacker pressure one offensive lineman.

We have effectively pressured offensive linemen by teaching the defensive linemen to make contact on one of the offender's shoulders, while the linebacker hugs tightly to the other shoulder (Figure 8-6). This initial contact by the defensive lineman occupies the blocker and usually commits the blocker to taking the defensive lineman. The offender's blocking commitment creates a weakness at the blocker's other shoulder. The linebacker has a blitz area between that weaker shoulder and the next offensive lineman.

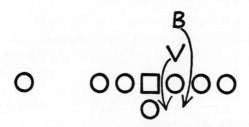

FIGURE 8–6

Occupying offensive linemen or crossing stunts is similar to another successful stunting technique: picking (or screening).

Our successful picking stunt has been a linebacker-guard stunt (from a guard stock alignment) with the guard picking for the linebacker (Figure 8-7). The stacked guard goes first and aims for the blocker's outside shoulder. The backer times his start for immediately after the guard crosses in front of him (Figure 8-8). This timing hides the linebacker from the interior linemen.

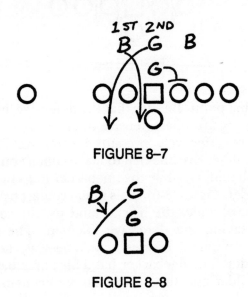

FIGURE 8-7

FIGURE 8-8

We use the stunt illustrated in Figure 8-7 when we are in a long yardage situation or prevent and we want to pressure the passer. We like to stunt the split-end side linebacker because:

1. The remaining linebacker can cover the tight end in the hook zone.
2. The split side of the offensive line has one less lineman to pick up the stunt.

Another timed pick stunt we use is the traditional two linebackers up the middle, off a cross (see Figure 8-9). The

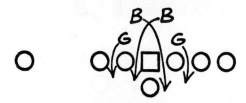

FIGURE 8–9

first crossing linebacker hides the second crossing linebacker and successful timing makes a successful stunt.

We use this stunt for middle pressure against a pass and run and for an occasional defense against the trap. It is effective against the trap because the backer's distance from the trap hole causes him to arrive after the trapping guard passes the hole.

Our favorite situation for the above stunt is an occasional first and ten, long yardage, and following a big defensive play. When we want to cross both linebackers up the middle, we'll cross one and have other backer merely check his assigned gap. He is then free to scrape on a run or drop toward the tight end on a pass. The gap that the blitzing linebacker slants into is determined by the opponent's run tendency (usually the tight-end side gap). This is also the situation when we send the better pass linebacker (possibly requiring switching alignment).

A double pick variation of this stunt that we use occasionally in a passing situation is to have the guards go inside behind the linebackers (Figure 8-10). Of course, if offensive line splits are too wide, this stunt is ineffective because the linebackers have too far to run to cover their gaps.

Another picking stunt that we have used successfully is a three-on-two stunt with the linebacker blitzing between defensive linemen (Figure 8-11). We run this stunt with our guard hitting head up on the offensive guard and our tackle hitting head up on the offensive tackle. While the offensive guard and tackle are being occupied, the linebacker blitzes through the vulnerable gap between them. After the

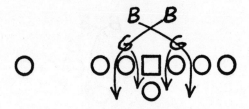

FIGURE 8–10

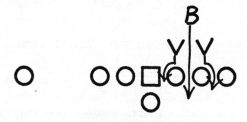

FIGURE 8–11

linebacker penetrates the gap, we widen our defensive line coverage by having the guard take a parallel step inside, and the tackle taking a parallel step outside.

We use this three-on-two double pick stunt as an indication of how well our opponents can pick up blitzes. When our opponent defends this stunt, we are not likely to be successful with any stunt.

Bluffing Stunts

Techniques for faking stunts should be part of your stunting package. If your linebackers can successfully bluff and decoy stunts, your opponent will have to defend you when you do stunt and also when you don't stunt. Your defensive play can become additionally effective if you can make your opponent defend a blitz when you don't blitz and not defend a blitz when you do blitz.

For example, our team has a reputation for blitzing the two linebackers up the middle. For our opponents to defend this stunt, they have to make interior blocking adjustments

when they read our middle blitz. These offensive adjustments necessitate considerable communication among the
center and offensive guards. Our opponent's communication usually causes a blocking scheme of both guards blocking toward the center or all three blocking right or left.

These two adjustments are sound blocking patterns—
when we are blitzing up the middle. But they are usually
poor blocking patterns when we are not stunting up the middle. If we can force our opponent into a blitz adjustment,
and we don't blitz, we have forced the offense to strengthen
itself where it doesn't have to strengthen itself, but more important to us, weaken itself where it should be strong.

Our linebackers recognize a successful bluff when they
hear communication among the center and guards that
changes blocking assignments. The linebackers learn to recognize the line call by the intensity of the language and by
the actual blocking scheme. When we learn the call, we fake
the middle blitz until we force the change.

When our middle blitz is live, we want the poise to look
like we are not stunting. We have found that this faking and
disguising blitzes takes two years to develop effectively. First-
year starters rarely have the poise to fade and disguise
blitzes. When our rookie linebackers blitz, they usually show
it prematurely because they want to assure themselves of
getting into their assigned gap.

When rookie linebackers fake a stunt, their fake is usually a quick jab step forward, followed by a retreat so that
they can get back to their assigned areas.

We have patterned ourselves to have our linebackers effectively fake and disguise every other year. This occurs because we generally replace graduating linebackers with jun-
ior linebackers. When a linebacker is playing his second
season, he has the confidence and experience to remain in
the line longer when he fakes, and to remain calm longer
when he blitzes.

To help our inexperienced linebackers bluff blitzes, we
add a "soft" call to most of our stunts. This call means that
linemen run their regular stunt, but the linebacker checks
only his assigned gap rather than penetrate it. For example,

off our linebackers up the middle stunt, we can call "soft" and have our linebackers check the gap each is assigned rather than stunt through it (Figure 8-12).

The bluffing "soft" call can be "double soft" (Figure 8-12 again), "one soft" (Figure 8-13), or "one soft, cross" (Figure 8-14). These three stunt variations (soft, double soft, and soft cross) give you built-in bluffs and disguises because offensive linemen have difficulty reading who is stunting and from where.

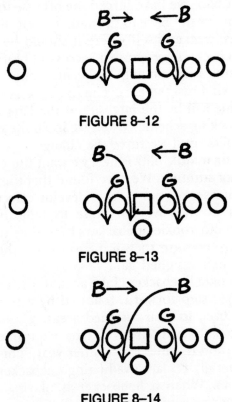

FIGURE 8–12

FIGURE 8–13

FIGURE 8–14

Ins and Outs

In and out stunts from a stacked linebacker and stacked lineman alignment are common defensive schemes, but this stunt pattern becomes more effective when the linebacker runs into the direction of the play.

For example, if you are using a stacked stunt on the offensive guard, and your opponent has a tendency to run the middle, your stunt will be more effective if the defensive lineman slants into the guard-tackle gap, and if the linebacker slants into the play gap (Figure 8-15).

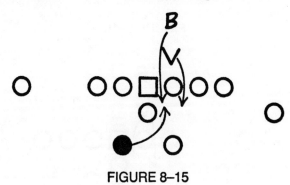

FIGURE 8–15

The advantages of sending the linebacker rather than the lineman into the play gap are:

1. The linebacker is usually the better player.
2. He has better vision of the play.
3. He's more difficult to block because of his running start.
4. He's partially hidden at the beginning of the play.

In most running situations, your stunt is more effective if you send your linebacker into the play gap.

In a passing situation, you have other considerations before deciding which direction to send the linebacker.

Some successful maneuvers we've used in passing situations include:

- Slanting an outside linebacker from the wide side (Figure 8-16)

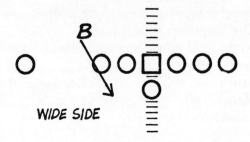

WIDE SIDE

FIGURE 8–16

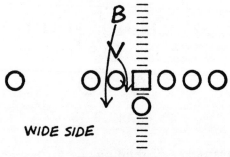

WIDE SIDE

FIGURE 8–17

- Slanting an inside linebacker into the wide side (see Figure 8-17)
- Slanting into the roll-tendency side of the quarterback (left-handed quarterbacks prefer rolling left, right-handed, right)
- Slanting into the passing side tendency (slot side, split-end side, favorite receiver side, etc.)

These pass-run considerations are especially applicable if you are stunting only one linebacker. You can effectively use that one linebacker to pressure the point of attack, and you can use another linebacker for pursuit or coverage.

Stunting to Pressure the Scrambling Passer

Pressuring a scrambling passer is usually more difficult than pressuring an agile ballcarrier because a ballcarrier wants to gain yardage, whereas a passer wants to avoid a tackler. Also, the scrambler has more field space to maneuver.

Before deciding where to stunt to pressure the scrambler, you first have to scout the scrambler's tendencies. Does he scramble:

- to and away from his throwing hand?
- to and away from the strength of the formation?
- to and away from his favorite receiver?
- short and wide side?
- right and left side?
- outside and inside?

If your answer to all the above is yes, you have a problem.

To defend a scrambler who is human, determine what he can and can't do, and pressure similar to the following:

1. If he does not have a tendency to scramble up the middle, outside pressure (toward the passer's favorite throwing or rolling side) is usually effective.
2. If he is a stay-in-the-pocket passer, middle pressure is usually more direct than outside pressure.
3. If pressure from one area is not effective, pressure from additional areas may be necessary.

Effective pressure does not have to result in a sack. If your linebacker pressure can force the passer to throw from an unnatural position, your pressure is effective. An unnatural throwing position may include:

releasing quicker

throwing over extended fingertips

throwing on the run

If your linebacker (or other defender) has a clear shot at the passer, the tackle should be made from the top down.

This tackling technique keeps the defender's hands in front of the passer and permits the opportunity to tackle the ball.

Tackling a scrambling passer is more difficult than tackling a ballcarrier because passers are usually more skilled, more mobile, and less afraid to take a loss. To tackle a passer, a linebacker frequently has to grab the passer's shoulder pads at the necks or grab his pants at the waist.

Trying to catch a scrambling passer is also difficult because of a favorite decoy move common to many scramblers. Scramblers like to tuck the ball and fake a middle run, causing an outside pursuer to take an inside angle to cut him off. When the defender starts inside and loses his outside leverage, the scrambler circles back around the defender and escapes the contain defensive (Figure 8-18).

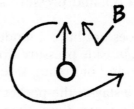

FIGURE 8–18

To defend against this move, your contain men have to sustain outside leverage by keeping a position that allows making the tackle on the passer's outside shoulder. If your inside defenders keep their rush lanes and your outside defenders keep leverage, the scrambler will have nowhere to scramble.

Under these circumstances, an additional pressuring linebacker can be extremely effective. Stunting to pressure the scrambler will complement the remainder of your stunting game and add to the effectiveness of your defensive package.

9

PREPARING LINEBACKERS FOR GAMES

The linebacker stunts described in chapter 8 include general skills that you must teach before you begin playing games. Summer practice means extensive teaching and drilling of your defensive playbook. Also, your early season scrimmages should include using all your stunts in game conditions.

Whereas your summer schedule includes learning and practicing all linebacker skills and stunts, your game preparation includes reviewing and refining techniques and stunts that are included in your weekly game plan. Deciding which material to include and exclude is what makes winning coaches win and losing coaches try harder.

Studying Offenses

To prepare your linebackers effectively for games, you have to teach them (and other defensive players) the intricacies of each opponent's offense. You learn these characteristics by scouting your opponents for tendencies. Analyze what they do best and how and when they do it. This information comes from charting your opponent's every play for three or four games or as many games as possible to scout prior to your playing them. Break down those plays and look for tendencies that show:

- the hole they attack most
- the side they run more
- the formation they run from and pass from most
- the offensive blocker they run over most
- the back that carries the ball most
- hash-mark preferences
- field position preferences
- situation preferences

At Sun Valley, each assistant coach scouts for his coaching responsibility. Mike scouts for his defensive secondary area (primarily passing) and I scout for the defensive line and linebacker area. When we scout future opponents playing each other, we scout both offenses. Head coach Bob Fithian and offensive coaches Bill Benedict and Ron Withelder scout both defenses.

The form I use for scouting my area is very simple—a lined sheet of paper. I write each play on a line. A sample line may look like the following:

1–10 60 Pr S swp R #46 Gs pl cts bk +8

Develop a shorthand code that you can later translate. To our staff, the above line represents the following:

1–10 = down and distance
60 = yards for a touchdown
L = ball spotted on the left hash mark

Pr = Pro formation right (tight-end right)
S = backs split
swp R = sweep play right
#46 = the ballcarrier's number
Gs pl = guards pulled
cts bk = the ballcarrier cut back
+8 = the result of the play

Any other significant notes can easily be added to the line. The advantage of this scouting style is that the writing takes less time than diagramming and one coach can do it.

Analyzing this scouted information tells you what your opponent has done in the past and gives you guidelines for designing a game plan.

You may learn additional information from studying year-to-year scouting reports on a specific opponent. For example, you should prepare to defend any unusual plays that your opponent ran two, three, or four years ago. Remember to also scout the coach. Does he frequently add something new offensively for your game?

Analyzing the scouting report and designing the game plan are usually completed before our Tuesday practice. At that practice, we distribute to our players a scouting report and game plan sheet. The original breakdowns and tendencies are written in a form that can easily be duplicated and understood.

Our scouting report also contains a brief evaluation of our last game. We list the evaluation under a "good" column and a "not-so-good" column. The "good" column usually has one more item than the "not-so-good" because we don't want to convince our players that they are not good.

We occasionally include on the scouting report any relevant newspaper clippings from our opponent's last game. This may include statistics or a coach or a player's quote.

When the scouting report is put together and the game plan formulated, the next step is to teach it to the players and practice it on the field.

Practicing Against Tendencies

We try to give our linebackers a scouting report during the school day Tuesday so they can briefly look it over before the other defensive players see it. This emphasizes the importance of their learning the report thoroughly.

At a pre-practice meeting on the field Tuesday, we review our past game and go over the scouting sheets. After talking about the information on the sheets, our scouting team (our irregulars) align in the formations our opponent has used. We want our linebackers and defense to study a visual image of the formations. We point out the numbers and positions of our opponent's key players.

After the visual presentation of the formations, the scout team walks through the opponent's plays. After all plays are shown, key plays are repeated.

Then our regulars walk through the defenses and stunts that are included in our game plan.

After our linebackers see the offense and review the defense, our scout team repeatedly runs a favorite play (full speed but no contact) as our defense runs each defense and stunt against that play. Then our scout team runs another play and we run through our defenses again.

We practice against our opponent's tendencies by telling each of our defensive areas what they have to do to stop each favorite play. For example, if our opponent runs a Wing T offense and has a tendency to run the inside trap, sweep, and counter, we tell (and list on the scouting report) our linebackers:

For Sun Valley to win, Joe and George (names of our inside linebackers) must:

1. stop the inside trap
2. pursue the wingside sweep
3. stop the wingback counter

List the plays you feel are the opponent's top three threats.

To defend those plays, you have to give your linebackers recognition keys for each play. You might tell them:

First, look for a trap blocking scheme.

Second, look for both guards pulling.

Third, listen for the defensive end yelling "reverse" if the wingback steps inside.

Ideally (not too many high school coaching conditions are ideal), each defensive group should practice against their specific keys and responsibilities.

But back to reality, emphasizing each area responsibility and running the defense against the scout team usually suffices.

Occasionally, you may want to quiz your players on their responsibilities and keys. If you find your players don't know how or what to stop, you need another method of teaching your tendencies and game plan—or you need an easier game plan.

You can teach your linebackers which plays to look for from which formation, but you don't necessarily have to teach situation tendencies, field position tendencies, and hash-mark tendencies. If you signal defenses from the sideline, a flexible communication system allows you to set your defenses against these three tendencies. For example, if your opponent has a tendency to sweep to the wide side, you should be able to call a defense that strengthens the wide side. Chapter 8 explains flexible defenses that allow you to defend tendencies.

In addition to running your game plan against your opponent's favorite plays, you also have to teach your linebackers to recognize special plays.

Preparing for Opponents' Special Plays

Part of your defensive preparation includes practicing against your opponent's special plays. These plays usually include screens, draws, quick pitches and reverses. These kinds of plays are usually run only a few times a game, but they are designed to be game-breakers.

Your linebacker preparation for defending these plays should include teaching the idiosyncracies that make each team's special plays different. After you scout the tendencies of each team's special plays, you have to teach your linebackers the keys peculiar to those plays.

Coaches have their favorite special plays that they like to run year after year. You must learn the kind of screen that each coach runs against you.

Screen peculiarities common to our opponents include screening:

1. To the short side of the field
2. Off the quarterback rolling the opposite way
3. To the back aligned opposite the screen side
4. After a 15-yard penalty
5. To a favorite, game-breaking back
6. Up the middle

Situation, formation, and field tendencies for screens can easily be analyzed and taught to your linebackers, but the peculiarities have to be drilled so that linebackers recognize the early keys.

For example, if your opponent screens off a roll the opposite way, your linebackers should be looking for another screen key when the quarterback rolls.

We teach similar special recognition keys for other special plays. To defend draws, we teach our linebackers to react to draw peculiarities such as drawing off sprint action.

Reverse play peculiarities include a wide receiver running a reverse pattern only when he will be handling the ball.

After analyzing all special play peculiarities, allocate a daily practice period (about ten minutes) for your scout team to run repetitiously all your opponent's special play keys and then complete plays. You want your linebackers to mentally visualize each special play. Then when they initially see a key, they will be reminded of the complete play.

Our scout team runs special plays and other segmented parts of our opponent's offense for two practices. During the third practice they run random plays from our opponent's complete offense. The final time our defense sees our opponent's offense is during our pregame meeting where our scout team walks through the opponent's offense as we point out keys for the last time.

Using Defensive Audibles

Occasionally your scouting analysis will reveal an offensive tendency so strong that you will want to play it almost 100 percent. This kind of tendency may include your opponent running one exclusive play when:

1. A player aligns in a specific location
2. The team aligns in a specific formation
3. The team has a specific situation (such as fourth and goal from the one)

Similar tendencies that we have charted over the years include:

- Running to the side of the dive back from a Power I
- Passing with the backs split in a Pro formation
- Running inside from the Pro I
- Passing from the shotgun or double wing
- Running an outside pass/run option when needing a game-deciding first down

When a formation or player alignment keys a strong offensive tendency, we have our quarterback-linebacker make a defensive call that automatics our defense to better defend what the offense is likely to do. We don't like to use more than two automatic defenses a game. The alignment we audible is predetermined and practiced.

The kind of defense we audible to usually involves one of our inside linebackers overloading to the tendency. For example, when one opponent likes to run off tackle from the Power I, our linebacker calls "Power I, Special 6 blast" and we run the defense diagrammed in Figure 9-1.

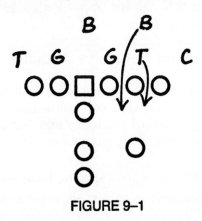

FIGURE 9–1

Adjusting to Game Situations

Your defensive game preparation should include your normal game plan, an alternate plan, and a desperation plan. In addition to being prepared, you must also be patient and give your primary plan the opportunity to succeed. Run your normal game plan until you are completely convinced it is ineffective.

When you adjust the game plan, try to strengthen your defense (when possible) by adjusting only your linebackers rather than changing the entire defense. By changing only linebackers, almost all your defense is still doing exactly what they practiced. Linebackers can usually handle adjustments better than defensive linemen can handle change.

The alternate game plan should include your preparation of adjustments to make if your normal plan doesn't stop what your opponent does best. For example, if you can't defend the inside dive area, you are going to have to sacrifice some defense in other areas so that you can strengthen the inside area.

Our first adjustment to defending an inside problem is an alignment and stunts that gives us four defenders on the three interior offensive linemen. We sacrifice some linebacker help in the off-tackle area.

The major game-plan adjustment we make to strengthen our inside is to switch our outside and inside defensive linemen so that our stronger defensive linemen are mismatched against usually smaller offensive guards. Of course we are sacrificing a mismatch off tackle, but you have to stop the water where the dam breaks.

When you make any adjustments, major or minor, make clear to your linebacker when you want an adjustment. For example, don't tell a linebacker to move from a head-up to a gap alignment unless you want him there in all defenses and in all situations, including second and one as well as third and thirteen. Your desperation plan has to include strengthening one area at the cost of risking defense in another area. Figure 9-2 shows a gambling defense designed to stop an off-tackle attack to the tight-end side. If your desperation defense doesn't stop your opponent in a specific area, raise the white flag and start building character.

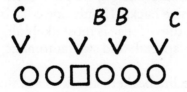

FIGURE 9–2

Teaching Recognition of Offensive Sets

Weekly game plan preparation includes teaching your linebackers to align and react according to how the offense aligns and reacts. Before your linebackers can react correctly, they have to align correctly. Inexperienced players frequently fail to recognize a variation of an offensive set. Multiple formations often confuse linebackers because they can't locate the tight end or offensive back whom they are assigned to key.

Also, many defensive players set according to the offensive alignment; a misaligned defender critically weakens the defense.

We teach our linebackers (and secondary) to recognize various offensive sets by drilling them to recognize:

- The numbers and physical appearance of the first two tight ends
- How many backs align in the backfield
- How many offensive linemen align on one side of the center
- How many wide receivers align on each side

For example, many of our defensive alignments and stunts are predicated on the tight end. As the opponent breaks the huddle, two or three of our defenders look for the tight end's number and watch the side where he aligns so that we can align.

As our linebackers align, we have them check the location of the offensive backs. If only one back is located behind the quarterback, the offense is most likely aligned in a double wing or similar spread and we automatic to a prepared spread defense.

Our outside linebackers check to see that twins or triplets aren't aligned on their side (which would also necessitate an automatic). We also teach them to look for the number of offense linemen on their side of the center. One or four offensive linemen on one side indicates an unbalanced line.

By giving your linebackers a checklist of variations to look for, you will reduce the difficulty of recognizing multiple offensive sets. In addition, linebackers' successful recognition of various sets will help prepare them to recognize the unexpected.

10

PREPARING LINEBACKERS FOR THE UNEXPECTED

Preparing to defend your opponent's tendencies challenges your coaching skills. Preparing to defend the unexpected challenges your coaching sanity.

Defending unexpected plays is difficult because you have to prepare your players to think as well as react.

Stopping Trick Plays

Preparing for special plays is similar to preparing for major offensive tendencies, but lack of time requires drilling your linebackers less against special plays than against common plays.

Your defense against trick plays is predicated on your linebackers' early recognition of the keys. If a trick play is run from a special formation, the unusual alignment is an early key.

To defend unusual formations, your defensive game preparation should include a general "junk defense" for these situations. This kind of defense should include an alignment that:

- contains on the corners
- pressures inside
- pursues from the inside
- defends eligible receivers

In addition to defending such a defense, your preparation for defending unusual formations should include:

- teaching and practicing your junk defense during preseason
- reviewing that defense weekly during the season
- preparing against unusual formation and plays the opposing coach has used
- preparing against unusual formations and plays currently popular in your area and on television

Defending an unusual play from a trick formation is easier than defending a trick play from a standard formation because the different formation initially keys the unusual play. Usually only one or two plays are run from extreme formations, and when you defend these plays once in a game, coaches aren't likely to repeat them.

Sometimes your only clue that there may be a wild play is knowledge that the opposing coach usually runs a crazy play against you. Conversely, some of your opposing coaches may be too conservative to run an extremely unusual play. Knowing the personality of the opposing coach helps you know the tendency, but always be prepared and always expect the unexpected.

Unexpected trick plays from standard formations (double reverses, double passes, deceptive handoffs, flea flickers, guards around, etc.) are not as easily recognizable but are still keyable. Some common keys for these kinds of plays include:

- extremely long yardage
- desperate need of a first down or score
- time running out and trailing
- 60 or more yards needed for a crucial score

Chart the situation and game conditions that your opposing coach has used for this type of play. If he had success with these plays, you can expect them to be used again.

You can prepare your linebackers to defend these kinds of trick plays by teaching them to recognize special keys such as:

- a wide receiver running back inside
- an offensive player varying his alignment
- unusual offensive play-action (such as falling and getting up)
- one or two players running an unusual play pattern (such as the quarterback running a pass pattern after handing off)

Experienced linebackers are often credited with the ability to diagnose trick plays quickly. This is a coachable skill that you can teach your linebackers by drilling the keys for recognizing trick plays.

Another defense for a trick formation is calling time-out. Instruct your linebackers to call time out for any unusual formation in the first half. When you want this kind of time-out, delay calling it as long as possible, to allow yourself time to study the formation.

In the second half, don't give your linebackers the freedom to call this kind of time-out because you may need to conserve the time-outs for your offense.

One trick play that you can't defend with a time-out in either half is the quarterback sneak run without a cadence.

Stopping the Silent Sneak

The quarterback sneak should be feared as much as any other offensive play. It is run with minimum ball-handling, it gains yardage quickly, and the ballcarrier has three blockers directly in front of him. Also, most defenders are designed to key a running back rather than a quarterback.

These are the difficulties of defending a normal quarterback sneak. But the offense gains an additional advantage when they run it unexpectedly without a cadence.

Similar to other trick plays, the first tendency for defending this play is knowledge that the coach previously ran it.

Another tendency is the situation in which it was run. Our scouting (over twenty years) shows that silent sneak situations are:

- extremely short yardage (1 to 1½ yards)
- inside the 10-yard line
- desperate need to continue a drive

We teach three recognizable keys for early linebacker reaction to the silent sneak:

1. Some quarterbacks start leaning forward before they receive the snap. Yes, leaning is illegal motion, but if you don't get 5 yards from it, at least get a key from it.

2. Some quarterbacks trigger the play by pressuring the tail of the center, causing the center's tail to raise.

3. The absence of the cadence that usually follows the quarterback's placing his hands under the center is a key.

Good habits of defensive play help defend the silent sneak. These principles include:

- teaching your inside linebackers and linemen to react to the first movement of the ball
- linebackers' periodically reminding interior linemen to watch for the silent sneak

This latter idea is a deceptive technique for defending other plays that you also fear. When the quarterback or opposing coach hears a player or a coach yell such words as: "Watch the silent sneak," "Watch the middle screen," or "Watch the bootleg," the offense coach usually reacts by thinking the play is expected and therefore defended. But defensive coaches, being more intelligent than offensive coaches (Ask a defensive coach!), know that the silent sneak, middle screen, and bootleg are always feared.

Defending Huddle-less Offenses

Another product of the creativity explosion of offensive coaches is running a series or a complete offense without a huddle. The offensive effort to pressure the defense is at the cost of also pressuring their offense.

Your first tendency for defending this hurry-up offense is history. Has the coach done it previously? Has any team in your area used it successfully?

Similar to defending trick plays, your preparation against the hurry-up should be practiced during the preseason and reviewed during the season.

Your game defense should include a time-out (if it follows the opening kickoff) and a variation of your two-minute defense. When the offense is trying to quickly align after a play, assign your offside defensive end to jog to a location about five yards behind the pile where the ball is dead. While this defensive end walks slowly and calmly back to his position, you have limited time to signal in a defense and your linebacker has time to call the defense.

Our experience in these situations has been that we have had time to signal in uncomplicated signs. We could also give our linebacker the option of calling stunts off our basic defense.

A simple defense is usually adequate because huddle-less offenses usually run a cycle of memorized plays. Look for a pattern.

If your opponent is calling their normal offense from the line of scrimmage, you should have enough time to signal in your normal defense.

Stopping the Clock

Conserving time and stopping the clock on defense is a skill that should be practiced as often as the offense practices their two-minute offense. Mental mistakes during this crucial part of the game often decide who wins and loses—and who sleeps at night and who yells at his wife.

Your end-of-the-game strategy must include deciding which player or players you permit to call time-out. Federation rules (for high schools) mandate an official asking you before the game who may call time-out—one player or all players.

We allow any player to call time-out because we frequently have a player on the sideline prepared to run to the nearest official and request a time-out.

Regardless of who calls time-out, your linebacker-quarterback needs drilling for *when* to call time-out. You can't effectively use the clock by telling your linebacker to call time-out when you signal time or to call time-out after the next play.

When you want to save time, decide after which down you want to call time-out and instruct your linebacker to request time from the nearest official immediately as the whistle signals the play dead. To be prudent in this situation, your linebacker must know if the clock was previously stopped prior to your time-out request and when it will start again.

In addition to a charged or official time-out linebackers must know that the clock stops for:

- ball going out-of-bounds
- incompleted forward pass
- score (don't forget a safety)
- fair catch
- illegally consuming time

Your linebacker must also know that a clock stopped for an official time-out (measurement, changing the ball, etc.) starts as soon as the official business is administered. In this situation, you would have to take a charged time out to stop the clock until the next snap.

Your linebacker should know that time stopped for a penalty does not mean that the clock will always stay stopped until the next snap. Starting the clock after a penalty is dictated by the previous play. If the previous play stopped the clock (incompleted pass, out-of-bounds, etc.), the clock remains stopped. If the play mandated the clock continuing, the clock will resume after the penalty is administered.

Your linebacker's knowledge of the clock rules will earn him the respect of his teammates. Chapter 11 discusses tips for making a linebacker a leader.

11

MAKING THE LINEBACKER A LEADER

Good leaders aren't as important as good linebackers, but if you can make a good linebacker an average leader, you have the nucleus of a good defense.

Our leader-less football teams at Sun Valley have been winning games for years because we have good players and to quote an opposing coach in a newspaper story prior to a game, "Sun Valley is always prepared."

We prefer having a player prepared to play rather than having a leader prepared to lead. But part of our game preparation includes training linebackers with leadership characteristics that spark the defense.

Teaching Leadership Characteristics

If a leader emerges from your defensive group, coach him similar to a successful punter—leave him alone. If a

131

leader doesn't emerge, teach leadership characteristics to a good linebacker. Confidentially tell him how leaders look, act, and talk. If you can't make him a good leader, at least you can make him a good example. Emphasize to your linebacker-quarterback the importance of:

- hustling
- learning football
- studying the game plan
- encouraging teammates
- playing with enthusiasm

Also, leaders usually dress better than the other players. Their uniforms fit well and look good. Leaders wear clean shoes (with laces tied) and matching socks (usually white). They have their shirts tucked in, and their shirt sleeves are nicely cut short. Somehow they have two sets of practice whites, so they have a clean outfit for every practice. Their hair is kept clean (and they usually have much more than the coach!).

A player exemplifies leadership by arriving at practice early and hustling to the field, finishing near the front of the team during running, being at the front of the line during drills, unassumingly carrying equipment on and off the field.

You can develop some of these characteristics in a linebacker by:

- giving him the opportunity to take charge of a small group within a drill
- initiating a drill around him, giving him the opportunity to be first
- giving him the responsibility of finishing a drill with one group while you begin with another group
- asking for his opinions about football problems

Calling Defenses

You want your linebacker-leader to display leadership when calling defenses—whether those calls are his calls or your calls signaled to him. His talking to the defense during games must generate confidence and excitement, similar to your talking to them. Showing confidence in your leader during practice will allow the defense to have confidence in him during games.

Your leader can earn player confidence when calling game defenses by following a few guidelines:

1. Speak loudly, clearly, and slowly.
2. Talk into the eyes of the other defensive players.
3. Flavor the calls with positive remarks.
4. Avoid making negative remarks.

Speaking slowly and clearly avoids communicating the feeling of panic. Inexperienced play-callers feel a need to rush the play-calling because they underestimate how much they can say in fifteen to twenty seconds.

Talking into the eyes of the players isn't only a good speaking habit; it allows players to read lips and see what's being said.

The play-caller's extemporaneous comments can add to (or detract from) the effectiveness of the call. Defensive performance can be strengthened with remarks such as: "This one will make you look good, Jeff." "We need a little extra on this one." "This is my favorite."

These play-calling tips are useful, but the secret to calling defenses is having good situations to make calls— situations like fourth and forty from the four, with four seconds left and a four-touchdown lead. Making good defensive calls in those situations makes you a good coach, and keeps everyone happy—players, boosters, etc. And you don't always know who is included in the et ceteras.

Coach and Linebacker
Communication

Your defensive lifeline is your communication system with your defensive quarterback. You need a communication system whether or not you signal in defenses. In addition to signaling defenses, your game communication must include sign language for:

- accepting or rejecting a penalty
- reminding to watch for a specific play
- running a prevent or other special defense
- activating a two-minute defense

Any sign system for defenses should be logical, simple, and unique. Remember that your signs have to be read from 20 yards away to about 40 yards away. The farther your captain is away from you, the more important the sign.

Avoid using any sign that looks like a time-out sign. Include signs for your punt returns and kick blocks. Make sure that more than one player knows your signs and review your signs prior to each game.

If your signal system includes right-hand and left-hand communication, think about distinguishing your right hand from your left hand. For example, if you wear a strip of white tape around your right wrist, your signal caller can associate white with right.

When you devise your signal system, use the KISS technique—keep it short and simple.

12

DRILLS FOR DEVELOPING LINEBACKERS

Don't underestimate the value of your drills. They are your major teaching materials. You cannot be an effective football teacher without good coaching materials.

In the classroom, you decide the skills your students need and use teaching materials to develop those skills. Coach your linebackers similarly. List the skills your linebackers need to play effectively and design drills that develop those skills. For example, if you decide your linebackers should be able to catch a football, use drills that develop catching skills. If your linebackers don't practice catching regularly, how can you justify criticizing a player who misses an interception?

If you regularly drill catching the ball and your linebackers still can't catch, evaluate your catching drill. If you can't teach your linebackers to catch, recognize that as a coaching deficiency and teach them to better perform another skill. Admitting a deficiency is not a weakness. Players have limitations and so do coaches. Compensate for your liabilities by better developing your assets. If you think you are good at everything, you need more coaching experience.

Coaching experience helps you determine the skills your linebackers need to perform well. To develop this list extensively, talk to other coaches, specifically asking them: What do you think are the three most important skills necessary to be a good linebacker? (Asking for three helps focus on important skills.) Your answers will include:

- tackling
- reacting
- speed
- aggressiveness
- agility
- reacting

- shedding
- pursuing
- football knowledge
- discipline
- ball-handling
- pass defending

When you complete your list, prioritize it. What is a linebacker's most important skill? Which skills must be skilled daily? twice a week? once a week? during the preseason?

Our prioritized list of linebacker skills (subject to argument) includes:

1. reacting (diagnosing)
2. tackling
3. shedding
4. agility

These are the skills we practice daily, from the first practice in August to pregame before our Thanksgiving Day game. Some skills are practiced regularly and others are practiced occasionally. For example, we drill linebackers on pass defending and pursuing once a week.

Reacting

Quick-reacting linebackers aren't born, they're drilled to read a key and then react to it. Reacting (diagnosing) is a mental and physical skill. The mental part (keying and diagnosing) can be taught; the reacting part is directly related to the linebacker's athletic ability.

Our daily reacting drills consist of drilling keys common to many opponents and keys common to specific opponents. Our general reaction drill for an inside linebacker keying a dive back is the linebacker assuming his position with the coach aligning across from the linebacker. The coach simulates the dive back and the linebacker reacts to the first step of the coach. Figure 12-1 is a partial example of the keys and reactions a right inside linebacker would use against a dive back in a Pro formation. The complete keys are explained in detail in chapter 7.

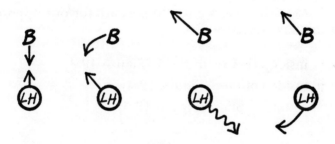

FIGURE 12–1

During the season, we drill daily against our next opponent's keys. If our opponent runs an inside cross (and the second crossing back always gets the ball), we drill our right inside linebacker to look to the opposite back when his key crosses (Figure 12-2).

If our opponent runs a Veer and our linebacker has the dive, we drill the linebacker to react to the first step of the dive back coming to him. We tell that linebacker to tackle the dive back with his inside shoulder, keeping the outside arm free for pursuit (see chapter 7).

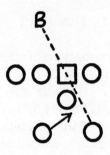

FIGURE 12–2

If our opponent runs a quick pitch (with a trap off to the same side), we drill our inside linebacker to react outside when he sees the ball go outside.

We run a similar reaction drill for every opponent's play we respect. We limit the drill participants to the linebacker and his keys. Occasionally, we use some of these key drills during our pregame.

These drills that we use to prepare for our opponent's favorite plays include:

- inside cross from the I (Figure 12-3)
- inside counter (Figure 12-4)
- counter option (Figure 12-5)

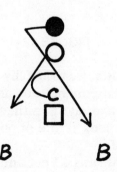

FIGURE 12–3

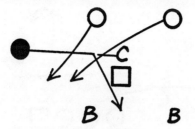

FIGURE 12–4

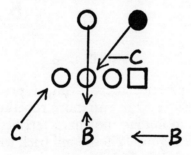

FIGURE 12–5

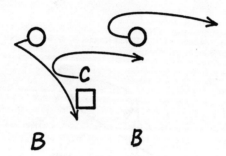

FIGURE 12–6

- power off-tackle (Figure 12-6)
- screens (Figure 12-7)
- off-tackle cutback (Figure 12-8)
- tight end quick pass

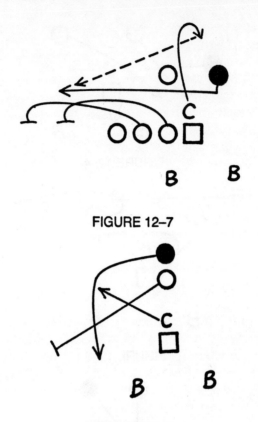

FIGURE 12–7

FIGURE 12–8

When we practice these drills, I prefer playing the quarterback because I can run more repetitions and tell the offensive backs to imitate the characteristics that I scouted. For example, in Figure 12-3 the tail back will often jab step right before going left. If I scout him to jab, head fake, and throw out his right hand, I can tell the back each play to imitate those movements.

In each of these drills, we practice our linebackers' complete reactions to their keys. When we drill against the wingback counter (Figure 12-4), we train our backers to look for the wing coming inside when both backs dive without the ball (or whatever way the opponent runs it), and we train our backers to hold their ground when they hear our corner or tackle yell "verse." (We reduce the word reverse to one syllable because "verse" can be reacted to quicker than "re.")

When we drill the counter option (Figure 12-5), we emphasize the exact movements of each back and we stress peculiarities that show which back is getting the ball. If we can't discover a key for who is getting the ball, we settle for drilling movements that indicate the play. For example, on this counter option play, the optioned pitch back will take two steps right before turning and going left. If we fear this play, we'll drill our right inside backer to pursue laterally left, after his key takes his second step.

Another benefit of drilling favorite plays is familiarizing your linebackers with what your opponent does most often. Recognizing play patterns gives your linebackers security during games.

Similar to the inside linebackers, our corners are drilled daily for reactions to the tight end. They are drilled to penetrate 1 yard when the tight end blocks down and to drop into pass responsibility when the tight end releases.

This drill is followed with one that teaches reacting to the combination key of the tight end and near back. If the end blocks down and the back starts a path toward the corner, we drill the corner to take a collision course toward the back (Figure 12-9).

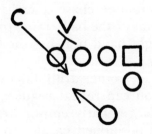

FIGURE 12–9

Tackling

Our second prioritized skill for linebackers is tackling. A football team must practice tackling as much as a baseball team must practice hitting. The ultimate objective of defensive football is tackling.

During summer practice we use a form-tackling drill. Each tackler (with a ballcarrier partner—no, we don't have a football for every ballcarrier) poses in the final position of a good tackler. We rate each pose from one to ten. If we have a ten, we use him as a demonstration model for the group. When we make corrections, we criticize only one or two points for each tackler. Telling a player to correct his back, arm, head, feet, and so forth is too much.

Our daily regular season tackling drill (not a contact drill) is run with two lines (about 5 yards apart) facing each other. We run a few minutes with the linebacker tackling the ballcarrier as the carrier approaches and then breaks to the right (Figure 12-10). This is followed by the carrier breaking left and then breaking to the side of his choice, with the tackler reading the break.

After breaking right, left, and randomly, the ballcarrier breaks upfield away from the tackler. The tackler chases the ballcarrier and hooks his hand into the back of the ballcarrier's shoulder pads. This drill is followed by an oral review of the techniques for desperation tackling.

About once a week, we run a variation of our tackling drill and have a defender chase a ballcarrier, punching through the back point of the ball, trying to cause a fumble. As the defender's right hand punches the ball, his left arm hooks the ballcarrier.

During tackling and other drills, limit your criticisms to short sayings that you can repeat regularly. For example, during tackling drills, regularly emphasize: "Squeeze your fingers!" and "Backs positioned parallel to the ground!"

During all tackling drills, especially emphasize corrections related to safety. If a player tackles with his head down, tell him you're going to put a warning on his helmet saying: "Caution, tackling may be hazardous to my health."

FIGURE 12–10

About once a week run a two-on-one team tackling drill. A tackler must shed a blocker and tackle a ballcarrier. This drill teaches shedding, reacting, and tackling. Linebackers aren't extremely successful during this drill because reaction time is extremely limited.

Another tackling drill that linebackers and other tacklers don't perform well in is a one-on-one, tackler-on-ballcarrier drill. If you have a non-linebacker tackle well one-on-one in the previous drill, you might think about making him a linebacker.

Shedding

The third important skill to develop in linebackers is shedding. A constant problem of our linebackers is that they hand-fight blockers when they should be pursuing. The quicker they shed blockers, the quicker they get to the ballcarrier.

The basis of our shedding drills is our daily "hitting drills." We aim to develop timing in hitting, just like a baseball player. Hitting a blocker with a shoulder (shedding) requires a linebacker, running, to make contact with a blocker, also running. The difficulty is similar to a baseball player having to run to hit a moving object.

We drill timing by having a group of seven linebackers (or other defenders) randomly deliver shoulder hits on our seven-man sled. Randomly hitting forces the defenders to hit a moving object (the sled's constant motion). Don't underestimate the need of young football players to develop timing and coordination for hitting with the shoulder and upper arm. We call this drill "hitting practice."

Agility

The fourth most important linebacker skill is agility. Almost all drills develop agility (quick hands and quick feet), but the importance of agility is emphasized in many teams by starting practice with a series of stretching and agility drills.

After our team stretches, we divide into our speciality groups with each group drilling their peculiar agility drills. Our agility is developed through a series of drills from a railroad tie design, with each player lying flat on the ground. Each player in turn gets up and runs down the ties in each of the following ways:

· in and out (Figure 12-11)

FIGURE 12–11

- over top of the tie, with one foot in each space
- over top, both feet in each space
- backward

Other drills for developing agility include any quick movements of the hands and feet.

Additional agility drills can be run during sprints. These include:

- spinning
- alternating running backward and forward
- falling and getting up again
- jumping while running
- quickly stopping and starting
- spinning 360 degrees around a hand pivoted on the ground

Ball-handling

Another drill that we practice every day, because it's fun and develops the hands, is ball-handling—especially catching and fumble recovery. If you don't like making some drills fun—make some fun drills. When we went to camp (that wasn't fun) we once ran a drill on a hot day where we aligned our players in twos and aimed then toward the woods. Each pair sprinted into the woods where we had two managers waiting for them with cold towels and cold sodas. Fifteen years later, those players talked more about that drill than they did about the games they won.

Ball-handling is our daily fun drill. Linebackers thrive on showing their catching abilities. Our ball-handling drills consist of each player catching a pass and recovering a fumble, while running to and away from the thrower. The thrower in these drills is often the linebacker we're trying to make a leader (see chapter 11). The incentive for catching the ball in these drills is doing grass drills when a ball is missed—that's also the fun.

Sometimes we combine ball-handling with conditioning. Our traditional conditioning drill for linebackers (and defensive linemen) is running a hill. We don't usually sprint the hill because we prefer continuous movement during conditioning. We use players' helmets to mark an up-and-down course (Figure 12-12). For conditioning we run the hill forward, backward, and shuffling. Our defensive tradition is to run the hill one minute daily for each point scored against us the previous week. The first day of summer practice we run the hill for any points scored against us the previous Thanksgiving. Our players look forward to shutouts, and extra points have a new significance.

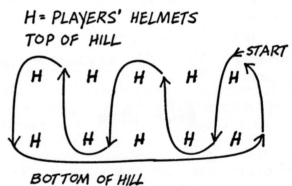

FIGURE 12–12

When running the hill for conditioning (not for points), we throw around a ball or two while running. If a player misses the ball, we stop and do ten grass drills (up-and-downs). When we first started this, the players were conservative and avoided throwing the ball long distances. As they became confident, they gambled more and threw the ball greater distances and threw it more boldly. This drill developed their willingness to take chances under pressure. As Shakespeare said, "Nothing ventured, nothing gained." Not being afraid to risk defeat is a formidable trait for defensive players, and throwing the ball while running the hill helps develop it.

Another ball-handling skill that we drill with our linebackers (and defensive linemen) is blocking punts and field goals (extra points) live. In addition to teaching the coaching points of picking up and running with the blocked punt, and so forth, we drill confidence to block a kicked ball.

The first few times we run this drill, I kick or punt the ball softly into their arms, to give players the feel or slight sting of blocking a kicked ball. Frequently this first drill is the initial experience many players have blocking a kicked ball. As the season progresses, we graduate to blocking a normally kicked ball. We run this drill by having each player solidly block one field goal and one punt.

Pursuing

In addition to developing ball-handling skills, linebackers have to develop pursuing. We drill our linebackers (with the complete defense) on pursuing daily during the preseason and weekly during the regular season. We start each drill by walking players to their assigned locations when the ball goes inside, off tackle, and outside.

A skeleton offensive team runs five plays: wide, off tackle, both sides, and up the middle. The defense reacts to the ball by running straight lines to their assigned locations. Figure 12-13 shows pursuit reactions to an outside play. A

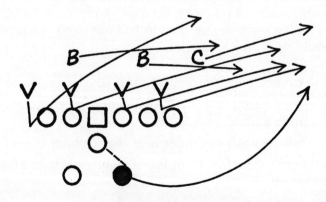

FIGURE 12–13

variation of this drill is placing blocking dummies in the pursuit path and teaching defenders to keep their eyes on the ballcarrier while stepping over bags. This latter skill is also taught during agility.

Another drill, emphasizing accurate pursuit angles, is a one-on-one, width-of-the-field pursuit. A ballcarrier aligns in the middle of the field about 15 yards from a defender. The ballcarrier tries to turn the corner on the defender (Figure 12-14). Coaching points for pursuit angles are discussed in chapter 5.

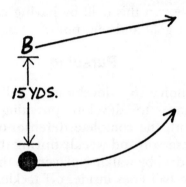

FIGURE 12–14

Stunting

Teach and refine your stunts by drilling them regularly and using only the positions directly involved. A simple, two-man (linebacker and lineman) in and out stunt can be drilled by teaching points such as:

- communication determining who goes where
- both reacting to the movement of the offensive lineman's hand
- where each defender aims for contact
- technique for stopping a play one hole from the stunt
- pursuit angles for an outside play
- situations that negate the stunt

One of our favorite stunt drills is working our linebackers and inside down linemen against offensive interior linemen. We can drill the linebacker stunt up the middle, with the guards slanting out (Figure 12-15) and we can stress intricate points such as:

- defenders slanting in on the ball's movement
- defenders slanting out on the offensive guard's movement
- backers hiding the blitz
- defensive linemen varying alignment
- backers twisting their shoulders when running through the offensive line
- linebackers crossing
- backers angling to a draw back in a passing situation

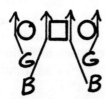

FIGURE 12–15

Pass Defending

We drill stunts such as Figure 12-15 against a running situation and a passing situation. Your allotment of linebacker drilling time for stunting and pass defending should be dictated by how much you stunt and how much you drop off. When we specialize with one stunting linebacker and one pass defending linebacker, we drill each linebacker accordingly.

A basic pass defense drill for linebackers is one-on-one coverage of receivers.

A drill for teaching coverage of the hook zone is positioning a linebacker in the middle alignment with a quarterback setting up and throwing a stop pass to either tight end

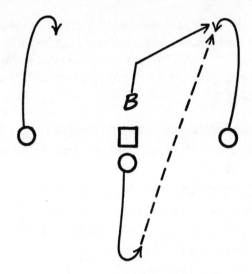

FIGURE 12–16

(Figure 12-16). The linebacker reacts to the quarterback's eyes and drops into the appropriate hook zone.

Another pass defense situation drill is having a linebacker cover a flare man and a tight end (Figure 12-17). The linebacker reacts to the passer, being cautious of not prematurely committing himself to the flare back. Coaching points for this and the previous drill are explained in chapter 6.

A pass defending positive-approach drill we use occasionally is conditioning linebackers to take a hit after intercepting a pass in the hook zone. We drop a linebacker into his hook zone, assimilate an interception, and designate a player with a dummy to contact the linebacker, while trying to make him fumble the ball.

Another category of drills that should be included in your coaching is drills with the primary purpose being fun. These drills don't have to be as involved (or expensive) as the "cold towel and soda drill," and you don't have to run a fun drill daily or even weekly, but when your experience tells you that your players need a mental break, have fun.

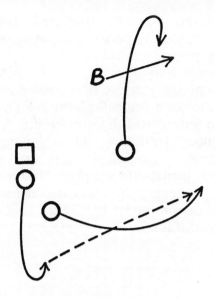

FIGURE 12–17

Examples of fun drills are:

1. Aligning three players with their backs to the colored pads on the seven-man sled, and quickly assigning each player a color pad to turn to and tackle.

2. Aligning two players on their hands and knees, facing each other helmet-to-helmet, with a ball on the ground between them. Each player tries to grab the ball when the coach takes his hand off the ball. (Caution: Coaches who run this drill must have quick hands or slow players.)

This drill will clearly show you which players have quick hands. Quick hand movement is necessary to free the hands from blockers and make a tackle. Slow-handed defensive players are a liability to your defensive because they will miss tackling ballcarriers who run close to them. This "grab 'em" also reinforces fumble recovery techniques.

3. Running relay races while carrying heavy bags.

These drills not only take the boredom out of the daily practice routine, but they also open communication lines with quiet players. You have an opportunity to see inside that X or O—and teach that person a lesson more important than winning a game.

Don't teach winning at any cost; football is a game, not a war. The supreme sacrifice of a soldier is his life; the supreme sacrifice of a football player is losing gracefully.

But winning gracefully is more fun than losing gracefully and good hard-hitting linebackers can help you be a graceful winner. Your defense wins the big games because your linebackers make the big plays. Drill your linebackers to make a big play every play, because successful defenses depend on successful linebackers. And successful linebackers produce successful seasons and make successful coaches.

General Index

Index of Keys